I0416140

MAN.EXE

Copyright © December 2023 Aleksandar Đorđević.

All rights reserved. No part of this publication may be reproduced, distributed, or transmitted in any form or by any means, including photocopying, recording, or other electronic or mechanical methods, without the prior written permission of the author, except in the case of brief quotations embodied in critical reviews and certain other noncommercial uses permitted by copyright law. For permission requests, write to the author, addressed at the address below.

Any references to historical events, real people, or real places are used fictitiously. Names, characters, and places are products of the author's imagination.

Front cover image by Lexica AI.

Author contact details: Aleksandar Đorđević, Belgrade-Serbia, email: alecjonesbooks@gmail.com,

MAN . EXE

Aleksandar Đorđević

To my wife Sofija, my daughter Anastasija, and my son Luka, wonderful people they will become one day, to ancestors and descendants.

CONTENT:

"How It Should Be"

At 20:58, while I'm persuading my daughter to go to bed, because it's "bedtime," sticky and tired from today's walk at 35 degrees Celsius, changing diapers, three meals, and two snacks, I sat down at the laptop and decided to explain why I'm living the best years of my life.

I am sure there are plenty of dads like me, exhausted, bewildered middle-aged men with a superiority complex radiating in some imaginary version of themselves, hundreds of thousands, seemingly calm but actually "very dangerous." Of course, only if you step on their toes. Meanwhile, toes somehow grow serious calluses, and all our superpowers remain within us. A bunch of Clark Kents, rarely any Supermen, wandering proudly, motivational vampires just trying to survive the day.

You see, the life of real men, I call our kind real men, slightly exaggerated in the first words of this book but enough for us all to surely recognize ourselves in them, is divided into three crucial parts.

The first part, childhood, and adolescence, ends when you become parents. I intentionally don't specify the age because often some of us never finish this first phase of life. This doesn't mean their lives are less important or less interesting than ours, but simply that they don't live them "as it should be."

What does "as it should be" mean anyway? Actually, nothing, but also everything. It is the basic program of every man, MAN.EXE, something not learned, something instinctively instilled in our children. Every moment when we unconsciously tell our son not to cry like a girl, to be strong, to be a man. That program loads every time a male child prefers toy cars to dolls, when he defends his much older sister even though he knows he'll get beaten. Yes, I will probably be criticized by this modern generation that will say "this is not universal because, well, my son plays with dolls more than cars and is really a sweet child. I won't object if he decides one day that he's a non-binary Gender Bender." Yes, that really exists, but I'm ready to give a thoroughly non-conformist answer, as expected from His Majesty, The Dad.

Anyway, the first phase, the phase of Childhood, is not particularly tied to a young age but to a time without special obligations, a time of personal growth, development as a human, professional development, dating, love struggles, finding a life partner. This wonderful carefree phase lasts until the third month after conceiving your first child. Yes, I can determine with fairly good precision, almost to the day, when I entered the Dad phase. When I decided to exchange my convertible two-seater for a large sedan, all the way to the first sleepless nights thinking about how I will provide for this child, how I will continue my career, and whether I will be the dad she deserves. This last question, how many times have I asked it to myself, is the moment when a man's brain matures. Truly, such a change happens in our brains that we cannot recognize ourselves, a moment when we realize that someone is more important than ourselves, someone for whom we would give our lives, and with a smile on our faces. The innate MAN.EXE is activated again, which has always been there within us, guiding us to behave as it should be, because we are men.

The day I fell in love with my wife and the moment we said "yes" at the altar, I thought I would never love anyone like this in my life, that the two of us were the most important people in the world, and that no one would ever be able to change that. How wrong I was! Now I know that not only would I sacrifice my life but also hers for the life of our child, and not only that, but the whole world if necessary because parental love has no equal in anything you can imagine. Everything becomes mere attachment the day you become a parent; love for friends, family, you are ready to give up everything not for the life of the child but for some simplest ideals you want to teach your child. Others cannot always understand this, leading to conflicts with friends because you don't go out often or with family because they raised us in their way and we now do something very differently.

This moment is precisely the moment when your parents enter the third phase of their lives. When they finally are no longer moms and dads, when they stop being parents. They get a new, not at all uninteresting role, grandparents, but they lose their basic role, and that moment can be very difficult for a person, especially for a man, as for some thirty years on average, he had only one crucial role, the role of a dad. So now, all that decades-long work is put to the test.

My life was anything but carefree, born in times of wars and hyperinflation, families falling apart due to financial and PTSD reasons earned by standing in trenches and later in lines. The life that most of us Balkans had, but a life that made me strong.

"The Birth of a Man"

When do we become a man truly? Through birth or in some other moment in life? A male child is born, but a Man is built! An innate genetic predisposition to greatness that some utilize while others do not. However, much depends on how you live the life given to you. Whether you grow into a man or not depends on every step you take thorough your life, on every experience you gain, and on all the obstacles life puts in your path.

Each era has its own problems and difficulties. Personally, I believe that the present time is far more demanding and dangerous for men than ever before. Yes, we are not in trenches, bullets are not flying over our heads, but as a human species, we are existentially and psychologically threatened. Threatened as men. The entire value system that made us men is now being destroyed. The attempt to suppress "MAN.EXE," to shut it down, and subjugate it to something distorted and degenerative is clear. In today's world, Lancelot would be canceled, and the knights of the round table would be declared war criminals. It's as if men need to be reprogrammed and taught what it means to be a man, not by other men, the "proven alpha males with pedigrees," but by the system.

Doesn't the system need strong men with their own identity? Well... When you think about it, it all makes absolute sense; it just requires contemplation. Who led uprisings and wars, who was the one to protect his family? Of course, the man. Now that's not necessary; we have the police to protect us. Right? Why rebel and fight when we live in an ideal democracy, and not just us but everyone else in the globe? Therefore, there won't be a war. Right? Protecting and raising children is unnecessary; they are always in daycare, school, college—the system will take care of it. Your role is to be an obedient beta male, neither fully male nor female, an individual of the system that sustains itself through your existence, imposing opinions that fit the current supply and demand of goods and services.

When you think about it, unnatural alternatives have been found for everything: promiscuity instead of marriage, pets instead of children, fast food instead of the traditional diet, pornography instead of sex, school instead of family, an apartment instead of a house. Everything is designed to turn men into beings that bypass the rules of the fundamental "MAN.EXE" male code that defines us as men. I don't think there's a central authority dictating this, but that doesn't mean there aren't those who successfully use it to their advantage.

Society has progressed to the point of self-automation, surrendering a significant portion of its integrity and sovereignty to the system, or whatever we call it. Likewise, we are giving up of everything that made us individuals just to fit in this system, being special becomes anomaly and we all try to symbiotically fit in the system, living like in a human hive.

Of course, this leads to the demise of a society, and it's a scientifically proven fact. The "Universe 25" project is a case I usually point in order to explain our inevitable future.

In 1972, John Calhoun created a utopian society of mice, providing them with enough food and space but keeping them in one place, essentially equalizing the differences among all individuals. Does this sound familiar? In short, this utopia grew for a while; the mice happily reproduced, generations of mice lived in this universe without social roles, practically only functioning as consumers and, well, enjoying life. Then, at one point, the mice began to change, the colony's growth declined, reproduction almost completely ceased, mice turned to cannibalism, and chaos ensued in the colony until the last mouse died. The scientist concluded that the mice died twice—first when their spirit and society died, and second, well, physically. Although the experiment is an excellent example of what society can expect, I believe the conclusion is somewhat inaccurate. The mice didn't die because their society collapsed, but because they lost the individual differences that once made them a society.

The basic definition of society is that it consists of a group of individuals who share culture, relationships with each other, and with nature on a common territory. I intentionally use the term "individual" because of its meaning of uniqueness compared to a mere "entity" as a neutral number or unit. Therefore, the basic premise of a healthy society's existence is the diversity and uniqueness of its parts. However, this diversity and uniqueness must exist within religious, natural, and cultural boundaries. This means that forcibly and artificially created societal differences lead to its destruction. Universe 25 would not have survived even if they introduced two added cats; probably the result would have been the same, at least as far as the mice were concerned.

"Man.exe"

Restoring natural qualities to the individua's, returning to the original source code while allowing the development of individuality is the only way for the survival of society as a whole and the development of healthy individual differences among people. This original code is particularly evident in Freud's division of personality into id, ego, and superego. Specifically, the ID, at least in a significant part, should be understood as what I call the "MAN.EXE" basic male code—something archaic but incredibly important in the development of a man and establishing his successful role in society. I'm not saying that we all have to be barbarians, pumped with muscles, eating raw meat, and conquering Jerusalem in the name of Jesus Christ, but we must be aware of what makes us men and preserve that archaic essence because it is precisely that original code that forms the basis of our whole civilization.

Often, this new era tends to portray our basic male code as something distorted and degenerate, and the greatest struggle for the survival of civilization will actually come down to whether it is possible to preserve the male gender in its original form or not.

The needs of society are certainly different now. We don't hunt to feed the family; we don't fight against rival tribes, wild animals. However, the new era has presented us with new challenges that essentially represent that archaic struggle for survival, finding a partner, reproducing, and raising a family. The new facade of civilization is nothing more than a reduction to these few essential needs, even though in the multitude of modern human needs, we often cannot identify the most crucial ones.

"Hard times create strong men, strong men create good times, good times create weak men, weak men create hard times." —Michael Hopf

A very common quote circulating on the internet lately but one that represents the essence of the problem with our inherent male code. You see, besides programming us to fight for survival and protect our loved ones, "MAN.EXE" also programs us to maintain that well-being. A significant problem in men's behavior is that over time, generational relaxation, catering to the ego, superego, our id is putting us in a stagnant position. At some point, a man stops using the ID. Cheap substitutes for basic instincts prevail. That's when hard times are created, leading to the artificial transformation of men into entities of a society that lacks prosperity and tends towards stagnation, similar to the aforementioned mice from earlier.

In the history of our civilization, it's easy to notice patterns of the rise and fall of mighty civilizations. Egypt, Athens, Rome, Austro-Hungary, and so on. Strong men build a state with blood and steel, establish their position, create opulence and well-being, indulge in orgies, sensual pleasures, wine, food, psychoactive substances, until, at some point, their indulgence turns into apathy and eventually leads to the decline and collapse of civilization. For example, ancient Greeks spent centuries building a civilization only to see it break at its peak of power and prosperity, in chaos, sin, orgies, and gluttony, conquered by better men, not necessarily more cultured but "manlier." The ancient Stoic mindset was replaced by sin, and such a society could not survive. This pattern follows Rome, and soon, it seems, Western civilization. The existence of weapons of mass destruction only postpones the inevitable downfall, which will probably be even greater if we don't return to our original code and respect the differences nature has given us.

The precondition for the growth of civilization, a new step forward, has always been war. If we look at the last 150 years, we'll realize that in moments of the greatest social challenges, growth stagnation, society recovered through a new war, resulting in prosperity. Why is that?

Why can't society prosper in times of peace the way it does after major wars? The answer lies precisely in Michael Hopf's quote: Men forget their essence, become weak, and consequently, society becomes weak. The Industrial Revolution arose on the burned foundations of the struggle for independence and the American Civil War; we entered the nuclear age on the foundations of world wars, and the modern era on the foundations of the Cold War. The threat and human nature to create a way to protect their loved ones from the threat are conditions for any progress. If there is no external enemy, the system will seek an internal one to justify its existence, eventually leading to the breakdown of society as a whole. Indeed, we can see that troubles "bring us together," even at the smallest level—within a family, two brothers may fight each and every day, but the moment an external threat comes, they unite for mutual protection. When one family feels financial or any other type of threat, they stay together, fight to survive; problems and disagreements arise when living in prosperity.

Similarly, society, as long as there is a potential enemy, will strive for growth; when there's no enemy, it stagnates.

In the current moment of relative prosperity, we are starting to forget our male essence again and succumbing to equalization, turning into entities of a society without specific differentiation in the male-female relationship, which is the fundamental prerequisite for the existence of a relationship, family, and society.

Therefore, our basic line of differentiation from another human being is at the level of gender. Whether we are male, or female represents the basic level of differentiation and establishment of a relationship with another person. Other levels, such as religious, cultural, national, relate to higher levels of observation of us as individuals, our ego and superego. Regarding the basic human code, it's only crucial whether the person we're talking to is male or female. Of course, according to Freud, the ID is much more and encompasses the satisfaction of all human needs at the basic, instinctive level, but here we're talking about something else—the basic male program "MAN.EXE". Sometimes, I even think that Freud presented parts of the human personality quite simply and neutrally precisely because he did not make his conclusions based on the differentiation of male and female personalities but on the human personality as universal.

"The Devil is in marketing"

Matrix, system, new world order—there are many names for what is essentially an illusion of some shadow world government that controls humanity as a whole, trying to destroy the male gender, portraying it as something wrong and inhumane. Sometimes I too feel that someone from the shadows is bothered by everything masculine, attempting to subordinate the entire world to a new system of values, destroy the family, religion, man, indoctrinate us into believing that the way of life we currently lead is wrong, and equalize us on gender and other grounds.

I'm not a fan of conspiracy theories. I love physics, science; I've always wanted to understand nature as much as possible, hence the nature of man. However, I don't believe there is a central authority, an omnipotent person dictating how we should be, what to eat, what to wear, what to say, and think. In fact, I believe that we unconsciously do all this to ourselves, and I'll try to explain why.

Living for decades, actually since World War II-the last major reset, in relative prosperity, civilization has become lazy. Men are accustomed to a life without conflict, without hunger, without the need for physical development. Like when you eat well, and then lie down for a nap in the afternoon, you are not capable for work, for fight, you don't have need to develop skills, you are just fine and that's enough. However, even though there was no war, the economy had to work at full capacity to justify this consumerism, to make life as easy as possible for every individual, to have adequate substitutes for all the real needs of a human being. That's when marketing emerged as a science.

In its early days, marketing was oriented toward individual needs. Still, as humans tend to perfect everything they engage in and that falls within the sphere of their interests, as a kind of revelation, the idea arose that if marketing is used correctly, we can surpass individual needs and sell them something they don't need. Then marketing mutates and becomes something we now call the system, the matrix, or the new world order.

The moment they convinced us that a product we would never buy is essential, that's when the devil in marketing grew and realized that it no longer has to sell a product to customers, but perhaps it's easier to change customers to the extent that they crave the product themselves. From that moment on, we buy countless things that we will never need. Food that we will waste more than half, clothes that we will never wear, a new iPhone every year, a new car even though the old one functions perfectly well, a new computer, furniture, a new self because the old one is no longer "in." It changes our thoughts by playing with basic human principles of the pack, convinces us that it's normal to change our minds, wear a garbage bag, and pay hundreds of dollars for it, that it's normal to change gender daily, equalizes us as human beings, and turns us into entities just because it's easier to have a potential market of 7 billion instead of 3.5 billion. Women are becoming more like men, men more like women, and we as humans are turning into a well-coordinated beehive of fat worker bees.

How to fight against this? Against the demon that seeks to make slaves of us to the system? Just like an exorcist, by uttering its name! The moment we become aware that we are under its influence, that we have choices, when we recognize the methods it uses to subjugate us, then marketing loses its power. Moreover, knowing its methods, we as exceptional men, can use its magic and power.

Be aware of your environment and everything that happens around you. Very often, I see people running, caught up in their thoughts, business, and worries. People who don't see the strings that control their movements as if in a puppet theater. That's the matrix that many allude to—strings that control us and society as a whole.

Stop! Inhale the air; you'll smell the scents of perfume, gasoline, cigarettes. Look around; see billboards and advertisements for products you wouldn't normally notice, but you buy them as if enchanted. Listen to the environment; perhaps a gentleman in a suit will run past you, his shoes will loudly tap on the asphalt, a girl breaking up with her boyfriend over the latest phone, the earsplitting sound of a Maserati exhaust as it speeds through the crowd at 20 miles per hour. Are all these your desires, wishes, and ambitions? How would you, if you were in the place of these merchants, improve the product and the offer, how would you sell it to these foolish people? Master the matrix because escaping from it is not possible; even the overly romanticized idea of leaving civilization and going into nature is a marketing trick. Speaking of the Matrix movie, I believe most have seen it; don't be Neo, be the Architect, or at least Agent Smith. Choose your battles until the moment of the new reset, which you will be aware of and ready for this time.

A man must be aware of his environment. Instinctively, he must recognize an attack. In today's society, where it's rare for someone to physically attack you on the street, as society has evolved from primitive times, attacks are different, more sophisticated. A true man is aware of his environment and rules his space. He transfers this awareness to his family, whose primary protector he is. Hence, it is the sacred duty of a man in today's time to instill normal, natural values in his easily indoctrinated children and protect them from deception and bad influences. This is the only way to preserve the family as the basic unit of society.

What does a man need to do to be naturally masculine? Unfortunately, if we have to ask this question, we are already facing a significant social problem. Looking at the generations that are coming, I often have to notice that all traditionally masculine characteristics are slowly being destroyed, declared wrong, sick, not modern, and dangerous. The traditional man is "dangerous" because he has strength, a healthy sexual drive, his identity. Such a man is a threat to society and the system that seeks to equalize all individuals to simplify and equalize their needs.

When I was a kid, it was elementary that each of my friends trained or was at least very active. We played football, basketball, tennis, and even volleyball. Today's generations spend hours and hours watching phones, playing games, on TikTok... I catch myself spending hours watching reels on Instagram also. As a result, generations are obese, not physically capable of withstanding any effort, let alone fighting, protecting themselves and their loved ones. The level of testosterone in future generations decreases every year, an incredible 1% per year. Finnish studies have found that from 2006 to 2019, the testosterone level has dropped an incredible 10% in all categories of men. However, this is not the worst; the quality of sperm has also sharply declined in newer generations, but there has been a sharp increase in testicular cancer. So, the lifestyle of young generations but also of civilization in general leads to the loss of basic male characteristics both in appearance and on a biological level.

"The Great Reset"

It's time for the great reset. We will return to the default version of ourselves. This may not be easy for some of you, which brings us to the first lesson.

You have power only over your thoughts, not external events; understand this, and you will find strength. - Marcus Aurelius

The fundamental factor in everything that happens to us is our thoughts. We often say, 'As your thoughts are, so is your life,' and that is indeed true. We can influence only our interpretation of reality. What is reality, anyway? If we start with the fact that an atom is composed of 90% empty space, molecules are made up of atoms, and, of course, the vast majority of empty space, and considering that all the cells in our being contain a large percentage of empty space, we come to the fact that the human body consists of almost 99% empty space, not just the body, but everything material. That 1% represents what is and what we interact with. On the other hand, biologically speaking, the perception of this reality is done through our senses—sight, hearing, touch, etc. As each of us is different, with experiential and other differences of a religious, cultural, and biological nature, each of us perceives reality differently. For example, a color-blind person will perceive reality differently from a person with normal vision. A highly religious person will attribute religious concepts to certain things and occurrences. Reality is not constant; we create reality, interpret reality, and various versions of reality simultaneously exist in each being. Thus, only our interpretation of events and things shapes our version of reality. On the other hand, our brain is not a hard drive where we store recordings of our past. Scientifically proven is the fact that we don't actually remember events; we recreate events every time we remember something. Every time, we recreate events in our minds, and each time they are slightly different. Moreover, if we convince ourselves that something different happened in that past moment, we will easily create a new version of the past.

In this observation lies the space for the development of us as human beings. We are the creators of our reality and our past, and as such, we have the power to change it, thereby changing what others feel about us.

For example, John had significant problems with acne in his youth. He was mocked in the school class he attended. His first love rejected him in front of the whole class when he expressed his affection. Since then, John developed a strong aversion to women, fearing to approach them, thinking they were all the same. In his version of reality, he felt unworthy, even developing a degree of hatred towards women. Of course, like everyone else, he always wanted to meet a kindred spirit and be happy. On the other hand, Jill grew up in relatively normal circumstances, had long-term relationships where she experienced love and affection towards both her boyfriends and vice versa. John meets Jill at a house party. John wrongly assesses that Jill's interest in him is aimed at hurting and mocking him. He becomes cold and reserved towards her, even repellent, although he likes Jill. After the party, he goes home without any contact with Jill.

In this simulation, which unfortunately is not impossible, but very realistic in today's world, John may have missed the chance to meet the love of his life by not realizing that his reaction and thoughts about external factors prevented him from doing so.

We must become masters of our thoughts and attitudes. Try to understand why we have certain attitudes, and in the absence of a solution, ask ourselves one question, 'What would the prototypical man, neandertal men, do?' In the example given, John should have asked himself what a basic version of a man would do. Of course, the answer to this question is that Jill is a female, Jill is beautiful, Jill is at a suitable age for reproduction, he should get to know her and explore the possibilities of starting a family. This may sound a bit rough, neanderthal-like if that's even a word, but it really works. Of course, this relationship will later gain its depth, depth of relation, common interests, and the complementarity of the couple explored through the ego and the superego.

Perhaps Jill is not really suitable for John, but John will never find out if he doesn't explore it. Not only in male-female relationships but in all other relationships.

For example, a high school student faces bullying behavior from classmates every day. He had similar experiences in elementary school. His parents told him not to fight. He developed a fear of bullies but was drawn to them like a magnet. In his reality, he sees bullies as 'those who will be on the street in 20 years while "I am earning millions because I will finish college, and they won't do anything but indulge in alcohol and fail". "It is necessary to be calm for the next 10 years, not to fight because it is not good, and violence leads to nothing, and God sees everything." God sees nothing and is not interested in why some kid doesn't use his male predispositions which the same God gave him to fight for himself. If God exists at all, I believe he would side with the bully. Nor this oppressed kid will probably do anything meaningful for the next twenty years, neither will this bully succumb to alcohol and fail in ten years while the first one is studying. There is even a greater chance that he will succeed in life much more and better than the bullied one because he has that 'fight' within him to seize an opportunity and progress.

What is the solution? Of course, ask ourselves the question, 'What would the prototypical man do in this case?' First, he would start exercising, develop his body to the extent that other men are not a threat and that he can defend himself. Then the prototypical man would verbally protect his integrity, and if that doesn't work, he would resort to physical protection. Realistically, the bullying would probably stop the moment the bullied became strong enough to physically resist because he sends a clear signal that there are boundaries that must not be crossed.

Why do parents teach children wrong principles of self-protection? The first reason is that they don't want anything to happen to their children because the possibility of physically hurting a child is less acceptable than the possibility of psychological harm, even though that is absolutely wrong because psychological harm often leaves much greater consequences on a child's life than a possibility of broken nose. That child twenty years later would gladly trade a broken nose for years of abuse and the destruction of childhood.

The second reason is that children are mostly raised by mothers. Without belittling this lioness-like job, we must notice that a woman cannot understand the male perspective, just as the reverse is true. I don't try much to explain female psychology as it is impossible for me as a man. If we were to compare the instinctive way men and women react to these events, we would understand a diametrically opposite way of understanding conflicts.

Women rarely resort to violence. Firstly, they try to verbally solve problems, and in case of an unsolvable conflict, they are ready to use psychological violence. Even physical violence is resorted to as a form of psychological violence. Towards men, for example, a slap on a face will hurt more on a psychological than physical level and they are aware of it. Disheveled hair, which is often the appearance of physical conflicts between women, aims to belittle the opponent. Precisely from this nature, women, when resorting to murders, mostly use poisons, which is a well-known fact in criminology.

The man, on the other hand, reacts in a completely different way. He enters conflicts with an adversary with a cool head. Psychologically, his goal is to resolve the conflict fast and establish integrity, and in certain situations, to assert superiority over other men, presenting himself as a more suitable, larger man, archaically seen as a more desirable sexual partner. When a man engages in conflicts with women, he mostly experiences psychological violence because he is not programmed to use it in a manner similar to how women do. From a certain point, he resorts to physical violence when sufficiently provoked. Of course, there are situations where men initiate violence of both types, but we are not discussing the deviant behavior of an individual here; rather, it is reactive behavior we refer to, and one should be cautious in drawing distinctions. When a man engages in conflicts with another man, he aims to resolve the physical aspect of the conflict quickly, so he won't resort to scratching and pulling but rather attempt to incapacitate the other party through swift action.

There are historical moments that are incomprehensible from a woman's perspective, such as during the First World War when two sides engaged in bloody battles, trenches, bayonet charges, chest to chest fights, taking a "day off" to play a football match on no man's land, sitting, celebrating Christmas, laughing, and then returning to the trenches and the fight for a higher purpose because that's how it "should be". The physical response to conflict is a natural reaction for a man, and one shouldn't be overly afraid of it. A man who protects his integrity, preserves his psyche, and rejects an attack with his attitude even before it happens. A man doesn't like physical conflict. It is something that is sometimes necessary to protect the personal and relational integrity. A strong man, aware of his strength and power, conscious that he can kill with his own hands, will use violence much less then weaker man. Weaker men, like weaker and younger lions in a pack, aim for their integration as pack leaders, as more acceptable partners for reproduction, as someone who will better protect their lionesses and cubs. Of course, we are not lions, but similar principles can be observed in humans. Emotionally and weak men are particularly dangerous. For example, an abused boy throughout his schooling represents a threat to society, especially when he realizes that his reality was wrong, leading to deviant behavior, family violence, and even mass murders. At that moment, he should either accept the new reality or continue holding onto clearly incorrect beliefs, leading to deeper personal decline.

Therefore, a man should be stoic above all. He should adhere to the principle that everything is relative, that our reality is very likely not the same as the reality of other people, and seek answers in his primal MAN.EXE.

"Don't try to bend the spoon."

But why not go a step further than just understanding reality? A true man is stoic, interprets reality accurately, and responds to threats proportionally. An exceptional man goes one step further. He warps reality to suit his interests. The moment we become aware of our reality and our perception of reality, we can take a step further, go to the other extreme, and force our thoughts to perceive our reality in a certain way.

In the movie Matrix, Neo enters a room where a boy is bending a spoon with his mind. He gives the spoon to Neo, who tries to bend it with his mind but fails. Then the boy tells him not to try to bend the spoon because it's impossible; instead, he should try to understand the truth, that there is no spoon. As Neo tries to understand what the boy means, the boy continues, 'It's not the spoon that bends, it's yourself.' This is exactly what I'm talking about. By struggling to change everything around us, we fail to realize that it's enough to change ourselves, and the result will be an altered reality for us and even for others. In fact, the others don't exist; there are only reactions to our reality. The moment we realize this, we become masters of everything.

This is a powerful weapon that each of us possesses. As Marcus Aurelius stated, when we understand that we have power over our thoughts, then we will have real strength. Therefore, we cannot change external factors, or we can to a small extent but not efficiently enough to make a change in reality. On the other hand, we are complete masters of our thoughts, and as such, we can warp reality until that distorted reality becomes the only reality.

I used to mock people who use affirmations, calling those men losers because, well, I know exactly what is real and what is not. However, the truth is that I cannot know what reality is for someone else and what is over confidence. From this premise arises all the power of this , kind of, weapon. If someone behaves like a wealthy person and shows it to everyone, it is very likely that I will also think that this person is rich. Of course, warping reality must have a purpose. If the goal is to "swag around" and aimlessly imitate the rich without any basis in the person's abilities, this warping of reality will do more harm than good. If, however, that person has another goal, self-affirmation, achieving success, and striving to become rich, then warping reality will significantly help. He will strive for wealth, seek contact with important people, and constant conversations about business and money will recommend him as someone interested in success; his desire will lead him to the goal itself.

What is the difference between someone who has 1,000 euros in their account and someone who has a million? Actually, much, much smaller than between someone who has a million and someone who has a billion. So personal perception of the goal is not realistic; achieving a million will not bring prosperity. When and if we achieve a million, we will have the same problems as today, just of a slightly different nature. So why not twist reality a bit and push ourselves toward further goals with a warp drive.

I remember a moment in my daily struggle and path to success when driving a car and coming back from a not particularly financially lucrative trial in a distant city (because work must always be done, even when it doesn't bring much satisfaction), I listened to a podcast by a well-known speaker and influencer who said that all we have to do is want, say a hundred times every day that I will earn money that day, that I will achieve all my goals, and that it is enough. The goals will be achieved on their own. At that moment, tired and somewhat bored, I decided to try this, convince myself that I could earn enough money on this quite unsuccessful day, and that somehow the universe would send me someone who would open their wallet and pay me for my services. Convincing myself that I was worthy of this, and that the money would somehow miraculously come into my hands, and entering the second hour of persuasion, the phone rings. A pleasant voice on the other side asks if I can appear at the prosecutor's office in half an hour; it's about some criminal case. Still two hours away from Belgrade, minimum, if there are no roadworks. 'Well, I won't let this down the drain,' I told myself. 'This is money. I confirmed that ill be arriving in half an hour, aware that I cannot get there exactly on time, not even close. Excellent, the prosecutor is waiting for you. After 2 hours and 15 minutes, I arrive at the prosecutor's office; my client has not yet been brought in; we are waiting for an interpreter as well because he is a foreigner. I notice a confused man in the hallway looking at some papers, asking me where courtroom 609 is. Happy that in this first job I succeeded, I approach him energetically, 'Don't worry; I'll help you find who you're looking for.' I look at the papers, "questioning as a defendant". At that moment, the man opens up seeing the possibility of help. All in all, that day I cashed in almost two average Serbian salaries.

If I had behaved as I often did, apathetic and tired, I wouldn't have even noticed the call, wouldn't have listened to these crazy affirmations of a famous influencer, wouldn't have accepted the defense because realistically, I can't make it in half an hour, and it's not nice to lie, isn't it? And I certainly wouldn't have encountered a client from the hallway and solved his problem. The universe somehow found a way to reward this self-affirmation of mine. Actually, it's not about self-affirmation but about twisting reality to the extent that we persuade others that we are capable, but also persuade ourselves that we are worthy of success.

From that moment on, I don't enter the office until I convince myself that I am an exceptional and extremely successful young lawyer and that I deserve both money and success and fame. Admittedly, up to this point, I already firmly believe in this, but the extent of that belief is relative, as shown by the fact that there are probably hundreds of thousands more successful people than me, similar to the relationship between someone with 1,000 euros in their pocket, a millionaire, and a billionaire. However as successful and good you are at what you do, there are always many more successful than you, but that's precisely where the motivation for your fight lies! With that energy, I can always attract new clients and success. Law is the ideal example because a lawyer sells security, the assurance that resolving your dispute won't cost you too much, that you won't end up in jail, or if you have to, you'll be sure your lawyer will manage to get the best possible conditions for you. Self-confidence is, therefore, the most crucial characteristic of a lawyer, and in this example, we saw that it can and must be learned even on a bad day.

Often, that first impulse when something needs to be done, when action is needed, is the most challenging. How many times do we look in the mirror and tell ourselves, 'From Monday, I'm on a diet,' and of course, we never start the diet because that motivational impulse never convincingly pushes us to move.

"Every action is an impulsive action."

In order to achieve success and understand our behavior in general, we must realize that every action we take is impulsive. Yes, we may think about doing something for a long time, but until that impulse forces us to truly act, our thoughts are not reality but projections of possible reality. Then, usually in a moment, we make a decision to start a diet, a new job we've been planning for a long time, approach a girl we like, buy a new car, etc. We can sit and imagine ourselves in the body of a Greek God Apollo for months, and those thoughts, no matter how important they seem to us in making a decision to start exercising, are nothing compared to the impulse that will truly force us to exercise. That impulse can be as simple as noticing a well-built man on the street, being chased by a stray dog and realizing we can't run more than 10 meters, or the awkward moment when we need to bend down to tie our shoelaces. Every action is impulsive, and this is a valuable lesson for all those who are salespeople and those who want to achieve growth in their business. From the buyer's perspective, every purchase is also impulsive.

For example, I had been thinking about changing my car for a long time, even though my old car served me relatively well, and I don't care much about material things; I'm more realistic about it. If it works, looks decent, and, above all, gets the job done, I don't need the new stress and uncertainties of buying another car. This is absolutely wrong thinking and doesn't align with the principles I will outline in this book. One day, on one of my longer journeys from court to court, city to city, the window on the driver's side fell from the window lifter. I immediately stopped at a gas station, found a new car in the ads, and bought it two days later.

Is a broken window lifter a reason to change a car? No, of course not; the repair is 50 euros, if even that much. Still, it was the necessary impulse to make me change the car. I'm not saying that a car salesman should create an ad that says, 'Your window lifter broke, buy a new car.' However, understanding the fact that explaining how good a newer car is, how many horse power it has, how fast it accelerates, whether its engine is environmentally friendly or not, absolutely means nothing when it comes to the actual purchase. These are necessary criteria to sell a car—reliable, modern, beautiful, fast... But at the moment of sale, every buyer is an impulsive buyer, and if the cause of their impulse is correctly identified, it is possible to sell them any car.

Everything we do comes from some desire of ours, but to achieve it, an impulse is needed. Yes we desire to drive fast car, bam, we buy it because of fell window! It sounds funny but it's true.

What characterizes an impulse is that it occurs in a fraction of a second; there is not much thinking involved. It is a brain reaction, the secretion of hormones that puts us in a state to react. From the above, it is essential for every good salesperson to react immediately. In my career and conversations with potential clients, I know very well when one of them will take that necessary step and conclude a deal with my office. What I consider most important is to establish personal contact with the potential client, and if that is not possible, find a way to bring the potential client to the very act of deciding. As we said, an impulse happens in a fraction of a second, and if that moment is not used, it can easily lead to withdrawal. What is interesting but biologically explainable is that if the impulse is not used when it exists, each subsequent time it is harder to bring ourselves to a new impulse. Why is that? Our brain, as we said, secretes hormones that bring us to the excitement of doing something. If we really do it, the later hormonal reaction provides us with only satisfaction in what we have done. If we don't fulfill our intention, stagnation occurs, and cortisol is secreted. For example, we decided to start exercising on Monday, but already on Saturday, an impulse comes, which we miss for whatever reason. There is a greater chance that we will not start exercising on Monday after missing the impulse than if there hadn't been one. This is a natural reaction of the body, and we must be aware of it. In the second example, buying a car, if I had accidentally fixed the window lifter, I certainly wouldn't have changed the car for months. So, the satisfaction after the impulse was missing, and it is harder to reach a new one. For this reason, when we feel an impulse to start a business, to buy something, to solve love problems, etc., it is necessary to act immediately, not tomorrow, not in a week, but right away, get up, and act. This is an embedded reaction in our subconscious and in our original code as men—the so-called 'fight or flight' reflex. Today, of course, is not the time when we will fight with wild animals, but we can use our innate instincts in modern ways.

It is important to distinguish impulsive reactions from reactions to an impulse. The concept of impulsive reactions is often associated with something wrong, impetuous, without thinking. Here we are not talking about that kind of impulsivity, but about the fact that even well-thought-out plans will amount to nothing if this initial impulse for action does not appear.

Modern times pose many challenges for modern man. We have already said that the system aims for well-being, and from well-being, new ideas do not come; there is no development and progress. Why is that? We know from ourselves that when we eat well and then have a good glass of wine, we have no desire for anything except maybe to take a nap. Every indulgence to the body and satisfying the senses leads to a reward at the hormonal level, which again leads to lethargy. A modern man is not in danger for his life every day, is not in search of food, does not fear floods, natural disasters, and war with rival tribes. Consequently, a modern man is lethargic, suppresses developmental impulses only by rewarding himself with cheap substitutes for reality. How many of you spend days getting up at 10, having coffee, having a good breakfast at 11, playing a game or spending a few hours on your phone, then ordering a solid lunch, taking an afternoon nap, then it's time for going out, whether to go out or not, hm, maybe that's too much for today, I'll watch a movie instead, and then fall asleep or have sexual intercourse with partner, which satisfies you even more at the hormonal level? Such a man cannot succeed, although many will say that he has already succeeded. Still, this is no way to exceptional success, building ourselves as an exceptional man.

"Step by Step"

So, what needs to change in a man's behavior and everyday activities to deepen and activate his innate instincts and impulses? First of all, he must bring himself to a state of survival. We are not talking about literal survival, but about bringing our body and spirit to the edge of comfort.

Wake up at 5 instead of 10.

This advice has become somewhat cliché, with all kind of successful men almost racing to see who can wake up earlier. Despite that, the advice is genuinely good. Waking up early aligns better with the natural cycles of night and day for human beings. The first humans certainly didn't wander around in the dark in the wilderness; they sought the safety of a cave or shelter as the first light appeared. Waking up early also aims to put the body in a mild stress phase. Remember, stress is an ally; stress is good because progress arises from it. Early rising also gives us more time for work. Productivity has been proven to decline as the day progresses, and the longer we work, the less productive we become. If we have morning rituals like coffee, a hearty breakfast, etc., it's essential to minimize them. In Italy, there's a rule for drinking coffee fast, on foot, and I believe it's the best way to enjoy the popular drink with a few bites of pastry or fruit.

Early rising is crucial for another reason: every man in the world is in constant competition for dominance. We are in a continuous competition to see who will occupy the throne as the best, the fittest, the most successful, the most desirable. Even though we don't think about it every day, each of us ultimately aims to be the best, the most successful, and the most desirable. This struggle is the essence of masculinity, the competitive spirit that drives us even when it's clear that we may never achieve it. This competitive spirit is at the core of our MAN.EXE operating system, and without it, a man cannot be a real man. That's why every hour and every day we lose in a break means that someone else has gained an advantage over us in our constant struggle for dominance. If I, as a lawyer, the master of my destiny and success, decide to take a day off today, it won't just stop everybody and wait for me to continue the race tomorrow. It means that I am paying the price for that day off with my success, with lost money. A real man has no right to rest, happiness-satisfaction is achieved by making perfection of ourselves. Every day we finish satisfied with today's struggle is a successful day.

On the other hand, satisfaction and limits should be constantly pushed. If you are satisfied today with an income of 1000 euros, you must not be satisfied with the same income tomorrow, just raise the bar. All of this implies that part of your free time, the most productive part, when most people sleep, you work or spend your time as productively as possible.

I'm not a big fan of morning training; I prefer to exhaust myself just before sleep because it gives me a sense of absolute extraction of the last atom of energy, and thus a sense of fulfillment for the day. Still, you can use this period of a few hours before work for training, planning tasks and the week, for everything you would spend time on at work, preparing emails with delayed sending, planning and researching to solve cases, and many other things that are not social networks, and even social networks if you must, it's better when nobody is online than in the evening. Try to put yourself in the shoes of our neandertal and use the first twilight for sleep and rest; that's when your body rests best. Don't go to bed at midnight but much earlier. Observe your children and their behavior when they go to bed at 8 pm compared to midnight; children are still unburdened by trends and do things naturally following MAN.EXE and woMAN.EXE. Our bodies know best when to sleep and when to wake up, but unfortunately, our behavior and rhythm prevent it from behaving naturally, and everything that is unnatural creates an imbalance in human health and behavior.

Skip breakfast.

Breakfast is not actually necessary. If we want to restore our male instincts, breakfast will only slow us down in that. Imagine the most productive part of the day, the moment for action, the moment to succeed in business, and then we sit down and eat 3 fried eggs and bacon, then wash it down with juice, milk, or even beer. After such a meal, any desire to work ceases to exist; the brain is perfectly fine with how it is, and there is no urge to change anything. The concept of breakfast is relatively new in history. It was invented in the 16th century during the Tudor dynasty in England, and modern breakfast, including cereals, was invented in 1944 when the phrase 'Breakfast is the most important meal of the day' was first used in a marketing campaign for cereals. Breakfast was considered a sin at the time because it was seen as gluttony unnecessary for one man's survival. For most part of the history, people ate once, at most twice a day, and often once every few days. Most part of the history, human beings did not have what they have today, so it is possible to justify the lack of breakfast with a lack of food. Still, then we should ask why those who did have it—kings, nobles, those who really woke up at dawn and not at 10 am—did not have breakfast. You must reward the body when it deserves it. Like when you light a cigarette and have a glass of whiskey when you do a good job, or Hollywood-style after good sex. If you don't do it for hedonistic reasons and giving yourself a reward but when you are depressed and stressed, then you are incorrectly teaching your body to stay in a state

47

where it is rewarded. A significant number of people smoke a cigarette when stressed or drink when depressed, eat to mask some life problems with dopamine, leading to alcoholism, obesity, nicotine problems, and narcotics. Rewarding the body, mind, and spirit should be done when it deserves it. Otherwise, you are encouraging unconscious reactions of your body that lead to obesity, addiction problems, creating an imbalance in behavior. Giving chocolate to your body when you are depressed is like rewarding a child when it intentionally breaks a glass. I often compare us to children because children are the closest to MAN.EXE in their raw form, unspoiled by experience. Why are you doing something to yourself that you wouldn't do to your child, even though you love them more than yourself? You know it's not good; you know you're encouraging unwanted emotional reactions, and yet you do it. That's why the struggle with drug addiction, overeating, and alcoholism is primarily fought on a psychological and emotional level because mere separation from food, drink, and drugs is not a long-term solution to the problem.

Daily training

A man must work on his physical health and appearance. There is no strong man if he doesn't have enough strength to defend himself from a physical attack. We can have enough money and fame, but if we are not physically capable of defending and attacking in case of danger, then our psyche as a man is not in the right place. Of course, we won't fight wild animals, but the possibility of a fight has been the driving force of development since the early days of humanity. From the first tools, bow and arrow, protective walls, to today when we have all this modern weaponry. But modern weaponry is not a replacement for physical strength. As we can see, soldiers still do push-ups and run miles and miles every day. All that exercise is not necessary for someone who will sit in a chair and guide a drone to a target, but that exercise is a prerequisite for building the instinct of a man without which any form of defense is unthinkable. Daily training also leads to the formation of healthy habits. Not only that, but it also makes it easier to make difficult decisions. None of us men will say, 'I have nothing to do today; I'll go to the gym to lift pieces of iron because I like doing that.' No, lifting weights is hard; it's logical that we'll avoid it, but we don't do it because we like it but because it's necessary to be done to be the men we should be. The first impulse is the most challenging, and deciding to train is the most challenging. Let's forget the gym, which can be fun in various ways; let's take the habit of running 5 kilometers every day. A much more challenging workout, a much harder decision to start. Let's try that for a start. Leave this book for a moment, put on your sneakers, and go for a run. Let this book be the impulse that will ignite progress in you, progress toward a better, stronger man, healthy habits, and a healthy mind.

Mens sana in corpore sano.

Training is also something that shifts our comfort zone. Training is incredibly important not only for a man's health and appearance but also because it trains masculinity. A man is a man because very often he does things he doesn't want to, but he knows he should do them because that's what men do. I often quote Andrew Tate here, with whom I often disagree about the essence of male behavior and the source of male behavior: 'Real men don't do things they love or want to do, but things they should (must) do because they are men, because it's honorable, because it's their duty, because they owe it to their ancestors. Do you think the men on the Titanic wanted to stay on the sinking Titanic? No, we are men, we must stay, we are scared, but we must, it's our duty to save women and children first; it's a manly obligation. A real man controls himself.'

If the men on the Titanic didn't have MAN.EXE in them, they would easily have overcome and defeat women and children, taken the lifeboats, and fled first. Chivalry in them did not allow that, even at the cost of their lives. We can argue about whether they were good or bad people, but one thing is for sure, it didn't come from their goodness or education, but solely from the fact that they were men. They didn't sit down and decide how they would behave in the event of a sinking; their instinct reacted, without much thinking.

But training is hard; I don't have the desire for that... The most famous excuses we have surely told ourselves hundreds of times. So what, it's easier to lie down, it's easier not to groom oneself, not to shower, it's complicated to cook lunch, hard to go to work, tiring to make an effort for a relationship to succeed and adapt to someone because our opinions differ, exhausting to change diapers and wake up 10 times a night whenever the child cries, expensive to raise a living being and make a good person out of it—all of this requires much more energy, yet we do it because it's life, because we should do it. Training is also an integral part of living, it can be difficult and unwilling, but one shouldn't think too much about it. Yes, a warm home, a cup of hot chocolate, and a quality movie are a nicer choice than going to the gym on a snowy day, but it's not a replacement for it. We must not seek a substitute for training in other things. Replacing training with going out or watching a movie is like replacing work with going to a game. Yes, going to a game is more fun, but it doesn't serve the same purpose! The problem is also that people nowadays perceive sports and going to the gym as entertainment/going out, which is caused by the promotion and marketing of sports. Sports are not cool, they shouldn't be cool; our bodies and our health are not something we build for others, for Instagram, and trends, but for ourselves. The alternative to the gym is running, preparing firewood for winter, heavy physical work—anything that doesn't necessarily end with a selfie on Instagram. Exercise at home, do 100 push-ups, anything that exhausts your body and mind to the point where you have no strength for anything else, because how can you go to bed thinking that you can "pull an ox's tail (Serbian expresion)", how can you give your body rest when it's not tired, when you know you haven't done everything you could in one day, not only on a business, family, emotional level but also on a physical level. Only such a way of life leads to perfection because you always need to know that there is at least one person in the world who has used that last atom of strength to be better and more perfect. How does this not create discomfort for you?

Relationships with family

Relationships with a partner are very important for a man's mental health. A man needs to be a man and nothing more than that.

The meaning of 'manly' has been reduced to something bad and wrong in today's age, even violent. No, a man is not violent. A man is someone who has enough strength but who uses that strength in a chivalrous way. A man is someone who protects, contributes, develops a moral compass because he is calm enough to know that conflicts lead to a physical reaction in the end. This actually means that a man should not get involved in conflicts when he knows he is not right because ideally, it will lead to the physical reaction of another man. A man should be a stoic, take care of his well-being. A man should be a faithful husband because he earns the respect of his wife, a good father because he takes care of the family, the best dad because being a man does not mean that he won't prepare lunch for the kids, change diapers, bathe them, and put them to sleep because it's not bound by wrong teachings of what a man shouldn't do.

A man cares most about the respect of his partner. In relationships with a partner, he is often accused of not providing enough emotions and love, which is not true, of course. The love and emotions of a man and a woman are very different. Even in today's age, men compromise to please their partners, allowing themselves more emotions than what is naturally predetermined, and often pretend emotions, leading to a negative reaction from the partner. A man is ready to give his life for his partner at any moment; his love for his partner is genuine and sometimes instinctive because it comes from that basic MAN.EXE. In times of danger and threat, a man will not rationally stand in defense of his partner; he does it instinctively. The same goes for children, although the love for them is of a different nature.

A man is a protector, and best way to achieves closeness with his partner is through a sexual intercourse. On the other hand, women are more emotionally open, expressing closeness through emotional support. This often creates a point of conflict with the partner who says, 'You only care about sex, not me.' This is, of course, not true. In those moments, a man expresses the greatest closeness with his partner, something women can't understand. Also, conflicts often arise between men and women because men 'don't listen' when women talk about their emotional problems or when women show particular closeness to their partner. This is partially true from another reason, certainly not due to a lack of love for the partner. Men are programmed to act. When a woman, for example, tells a man about a problem she has with a colleague at work, just wanting him to listen, there isn't much empathy developing in the man's head; instead, he makes all possible scenarios of problem-solving. A man is a 'problem solver,' so you often hear him say things that women least want to hear in those moments, such as 'quit your job' or him being ready for a physical altercation with the one who bothers his partner. A man is often frustrated by such conversations because it comes from his basic nature of problem-solving; he simply cannot control himself to a great extent, listen to the problem, and not offer a solution but empathy. This is, of course, not because a man doesn't love his partner; quite the opposite, if he loves her, he will seek a solution.

The relationships of modern man with his children must be intimate. For hundreds of years, a father did not have to be with his children to be their role model. It was enough to be the head of the family, hunt, provide for the children, and protect them from others. Another man had no place near male, let alone female children. Today is different. Children do not find role models in their parents, and they are not difficult to come into contact with from other potential role models such as athletes, influencers, movie stars. The position of the father and dad is more threatened today than ever, and it's essential for every child. According to research in the United States in 1997, 70% of all juvenile delinquents came from fatherless families. Fatherless families accounted for 72% of juvenile murderers, 60% of juvenile rapists, 70% of teenage pregnancies, 70% of teenage suicides, 70% of running away from home, 63% of all suicides, 71% of drug addicts, 80% of later-life prisoners, 90% of all homeless minors. Children raised without fathers in the family have: 5 times more chances of committing suicide, 9 times more likely to drop out of school, 10 times more likely to use drugs, 14 times more likely to commit rape, 20 times more likely to end up in prison. 32 times more likely to run away from home. These are official statistics, which are just one part of the complex problem of the lack of a father figure in the family. A man in today's age must remain devoted to children, be a paternal figure, sometimes strict, but someone who will instill the right principles in them, those that mothers naturally cannot instill in children. Many women would now say that they are enough, that they gave birth to them, so they will raise them themselves. Still, it is enough to show this statistic to understand how significant the impact of the absence of the father in the family is. Mothers are wonderful, mothers give children a lot of things that fathers cannot, but there are things that only a father can provide. That's why a modern man is sometimes forced to spend more common time his children than he would otherwise have to. In the onslaught of all other possible role models, the father figure is lost, but a father doesn't have to fight to remain relevant. It's enough to be there when it's really needed, to be the pillar of the family.

To be exceptional men, we must understand our role in educating our children. We must sometimes be strict, instill family bonding rituals in children, going to church; it's the father who introduces religion to children. We must provide children with other role models, real ones, good and bad, and help them differentiate between them, take them to celebrations, family gatherings, teach them responsibility, care for others, teach them to set their red lines, and encourage them to defend them. But we must also be dads, understand our partners and go beyond the role of a father, attend childbirth because only then will we know the pain women go through to bring our children into the world, and at the same time create enormous respect for our women. This is how a healthy, strong, God-pleasing family is built. A family that will withstand the test of time and the system.

In today's world, as we can see, there are many substitutes for traditional values, and thus, education has been transferred to kindergartens and schools. A man must not allow institutional systems to educate his children; it is his sacred duty to provide moral guidance to his children. Never neglect the family because of work, entertainment, or anything else; the family is the basic unit and purpose of a man's existence. The purpose of work is somewhat to provide for the family and partly for the affirmation of male competitive personality and the development of the man as an individual.

Socializing

The social sphere of every man is imperative for the development of the male personality. Try to surround yourself with people with whom you will grow every day. Of course, I'm not saying that you should reject friendships, but you should certainly not stay with people at the level you met them. We often see that men maintain contacts even after becoming successful family men, with men who do not progress for years and decades, behaving delinquently, etc. The saying "you are the company you keep" very often describes the problem that such socializing creates. You must be aware that your friends, your acquaintances, create your personal but also objective impression of yourself. Associating with a local drug addict, even if he has never shown anything bad towards you, creates an impression that you are like him and undesirable in society.

The proto man, besides himself and his family, had to associate with more successful families in tribes to survive collectively. The tribe dealt with delinquent and ethically undesirable behavior through persecution or punishment. Therefore, a man who cares about himself and his future must build friendships with people better than himself because that is a precondition for progress. By "better," I mean more successful, wealthier, with more influence, with a good family, and good children who will not lead his children astray. There should be no empathy and pity regarding these choices, only objectivity.

When choosing friends, keep in mind that the topics of your conversations will reflect your aspirations in the future. If you, with friends, no matter how wealthy they are, sit and drink beer and talk about women, affairs, and similar "manly stories," such socializing can only create problems for your family and relationships with your partner. On the other hand, talking about ideals, jobs, experiences, etc., will lead you in a positive direction for further development.

Every successful man surrounds himself with successful friends; hence, the sayings "you are the company you keep." You must be surrounded by successful friends, share common interests, progress, and seek references in such relationships.

In Serbia, we used the term "domaćin" (host, patriarch, householder is closest by meaning in English), and it seems like a term that better defines what kind of man one should be – living with his family on his property, living off his work, respected in his environment and community, leading the home, devoted to the family, the head of the household, not hanging out in bars, whose word is respected and valued, defends home and family, fulfilling his duty in times of war, etc. The definition of a "domaćin" never existed, but everyone knew its meaning when they saw him. Today, it's very difficult to define what it means to be "domaćin", what qualities make a modern man a "domaćin", yet it seems that we recognize it in him, in his appearance, in how society treats him, in his demeanor. The "domaćin" is by no means a dead category, but unfortunately, there are fewer of them.

The problem that arises with middle-aged men is the loss of friendships and connections that once existed. We realize that it's much harder to find a friend than when, for example, we were 16 years old, and it was enough to play a football match with completely unknown kids to end up at each other's gatherings or go out together in the city. Middle-aged men have very limited time for socializing; families, children, and work are limiting factors that do not allow us to maintain relationships with other people at a high quality. How often do you ask yourself, "How long has it been since I saw this friend? It's been at least 3 months." We must understand that this is entirely normal given our obligations but that we must do everything in our power to maintain friendships, quality friendships, of course. Instead of focusing on one friend, try to organize group gatherings; this will save time and make it easier for those people to see you. Interest-based gatherings are not a substitute for friendships but are just as necessary for your progress as a businessperson. Associations, seminars, fairs, any gathering that attracts a large number of potential business partners must be your obligation. Set a goal to attend at least one networking event per month or every three months; it will mean a lot to your business, and of course, always adjust your goals when you achieve them and grow, all the time.

Money

Money, apart from its role as a means of payment, is, above all, a measure of success for every man. Men are highly competitive and love to be more successful than other men, which is a derivative of our innate "MAN.EXE" program.

A man must be capable of earning money, taking care of his family, and nurturing his mental health in this way. Our nature, regarding providing for the family, primarily concerns ensuring our family has the means to survive. It's not surprising that some men stop at this point, merely surviving. How many times have you said to yourself, "Just enough to get through the month," or when you're a bit short of money, something happens, and you borrow somewhere, then end up having just enough to repay and survive the next period? Many will recognize themselves in this; unfortunately, I spent my childhood with a father who didn't understand this essential flaw in our male psyche. Without experiencing this limitation of the male psyche, myself, I probably couldn't understand what the problem was. On the other hand, as an adult, I deeply regret that he couldn't grasp this and lead a much carefree life. My father is also a lawyer, but he wasn't always one. Living in the countryside during sanctions and hyperinflation, agriculture replaced his beginnings in law. With hands in the soil and eyes toward the sky, fearing natural disasters, droughts, and other factors beyond our control, we started each year. I can freely say that these were the most stressful years of my life. Watching parents, adults trying to shield us, as children, from poverty and problems, crying broken in the hallway of our family home, watching the hailstorm as it destroys all crops... My sister and I, comforting them that something is still left, that we will plant something else and survive the winter... On the other hand, there were a few good years, but what always remained a big question mark, even after good and bad years, is why do we manage to survive every year? My father would often say, "God looked at us," or if something happened, "who knows how we would survive" — is the answer to this question is God, the universe, karma, or whatever inexplicable force? Or something else, more profound to our inner being?

Let's return once again to the Stoic view of reality; we can only control our thoughts, not external influences. Today, I understand that my father made only one mistake, a mistake that cost him nerves and youth, and that was a focus on survival. Indeed, my father always wanted to survive, and then if there's something left over... Of course, now I know from the start that there will never be anything left because the focus wasn't on that. How did he overcome this personal flaw and take a step forward? Unfortunately, I think he never took that step forward. Everything he did in his life; he did out of fear and the will to survive. When my sister and I were little, of course, our needs were much smaller and could be met through agriculture. At the moment of realization that two children, excellent students, all A in school, are embarking on the path of high school and then academic studies, this needs for significantly larger amounts of money then for mere survival, and it changed my father's thinking in that moment. He understood that it's time to return to law practice and that he must take a bit more risk than usual. The first years of practicing law were again about survival, then the situation improved, but new expenses came, studies, the lives of two students, new survival, etc. Every step forward was, in fact, conditioned by new survival. My marriage, even though I didn't plan it that way and my parents were invited as guests, brought my father to a new moment of survival - "I MUST pay for the wedding" (of course, he didn't), what if he doesn't have enough money to survive when grandchildren come, and so on, one spiral of fear and anxiety which newer ends. Regardless of the fact that all my father's fears in me were entirely unfounded, in his first year of law practice, I earned more than he did in his 15th year. Still, that fear always existed. That tension that didn't gave him the opportunity to spread his wings and escape from the survival zone. Please understand, there's no significant difference in having problems, between someone who has money and someone who doesn't; the more money you have, the greater your needs. Still, it's about how you view those needs, whether as someone barely surviving or giving yourself the opportunity to progress. I often try to explain to him where he's wrong, but as a proud man of the 20th century, he doesn't want to listen, so I often lose my temper in vain. My father also has the wrong attitude that what we can do is a maximum of 10%, and 90% are external factors.

As I mentioned, there are many such men today who live from paycheck to paycheck, surviving every month, and we always hear them complaining about the state, the system, people, how it's impossible to earn, how tax authority take everything, how the state hinders you, how everything is reserved only for "them.(someone close to government or criminals and so on)" In fact, this is a pattern of convincing oneself that everything happening to you isn't your fault but someone else's. In my father's case, it was the hailstorm, in the case of newer generations, it's the system, or the state. It's easy to blame the system or the state, but why have we never wondered who makes up that state or system? Of course, these are people, all of us, some are more skillful, some more "corrupt" if you will, although I personally don't call them that because I think that everybody has tools, it's the way you use it that matters. How can some people be at the top of the pyramid, and others at the bottom? Nobody wonders how they reached the top and what it takes to move from the bottom. Accepting the fact that everything happening to us is not at all our fault but due to circumstances beyond our control is the moment when we kill ourselves, our manhood, and our own progress. Opportunities are created; they don't come by themselves, and we must understand that to progress. Money as a measure of the value of everything we do in business is just a byproduct of our progress in a business sense.

Besides this type of men, there is a subgroup of men who subjectively do everything, but "nothing succeeds." Many will probably read this book. Often, I was also one of them until I introduced a control mechanism. So here we are talking about men who watch tutorials, read books, are full of motivation, do various things to develop a business, but again with no results. Ultimately, they fall into the same group mentioned earlier, developing resentment towards external factors because it's evidently not their fault but something external preventing them from progressing. Saturated market, monopolies, cartel behavior, competition, etc. The essence is that the vast majority of these people actually create an illusion, a super version of themselves, doing everything in their power, but objectively speaking, that "deed" is not relevant for objective growth.

When we notice that what we do in business has no effect, we must create a control mechanism, put ourselves in the position of a third party, and assess whether that third party could have feedback on our actions and what that feedback is. For example, about 6 years ago, I created a small cosmetic company. Like any business novice, I invested in production, quality, branding, money, money, money, a bit of marketing, produced large quantities, and then a bit more marketing. My idea was to have enough stock for 2 years, and the quality and the old name's brand recognition would do the rest. I listed my product in pharmacies, did what I thought was a good job, expected a return on investment in 3 years, and then pure profit. However, the most important thing is that I didn't look at my product through the eyes of third parties. All my investment, stress, and involvement in the first two years of work realistically could fit into a month of serious company work. To me, on the other hand, it looked like I was working 24 hours a day. Of course, there were not enough results. You could say I achieved the set goals, which were initially set wrong, but that's another story. In the end, due to the fact that I didn't have enough time to manage this company, I sold it. The epilogue of everything: I earned three times the invested amount, but I missed the opportunity to earn 30 times the investment because I didn't have mechanisms for self-assessment of my (non)work.

The first mistake: succeeding in cosmetics production when conglomerates have all kinds of products on the market is possible, but not in the short term. In other words, don't produce if the goal is profit and not brand building. The second mistake: never set goals so low; money must be earned immediately, not in three years. The best businessmen don't wait 3, 5, 10 years for a return on investment. When someone like Elon Musk starts a new business, he doesn't take 20,000 euros from his piggy bank, invests it in something, and hopes to return it in 5 years. Actually, he goes to the bank, takes out a loan, includes his work and earnings in the expenses, and pay himself first! The company is a separate legal entity, and that's how we should view it. Our work is not free and should not be free, which is a mistake all beginners make. The project includes not only covering costs to third parties but also to the founder, and, ultimately, the bank is the one with the best methods of determining whether the business is profitable or not.

What I advise clients when seeking my opinion on mergers or acquisitions of companies is to listen to what the bank thinks about it. Assuming the client doesn't have top-notch economists and advisors in this field, it's always safer to take over a business that was initially funded by a bank credits. Because for the bank to give the green light to project financing, this project had to go through the scrutiny of the risk assessment department.

The third mistake is personal involvement in jobs. Unless you're a lawyer partially tied to that job, an artist, soldier, doctor, and all those jobs that fall into personal professions, you must not personally tie yourself to the companies and brands you create. This is the most common cause of making bad decisions and the downfall of companies. Your goal should be profit; how quickly can I withdraw and how much. If this means having a company for only 2 months, that's fine if it brings immediate profit. Be cold mathematician when making business decisions, don't attach yourself to people or brands; everything is subject to change, you don't have to pay suppliers, you don't have to pay salaries, but you must prioritize your earnings, and then everything else follows. No supplier will make a problem if you delay payment for a month; it's actually expected in business. I have clients whose main principle is not to pay suppliers for at least three months after the invoice due date. The state doesn't pay anything without a three-month delay. Of course, all this depends on the system, but logically, everyone would rather wait a month than go through enforcement procedures that take 2 months. I know this sounds harsh, but business can be harsh sometimes. After that, it's time to pay the employees. You only pay employee salaries from the company's inflow, never from your pocket. Even a liquidity bank loan is always a better option when paying salaries than personal assistance to the company. We always must distinguish ourselves and companies and separate our assets. If there is no inflow, even then, a liquidity loan is an option for paying not only employees but also your own earnings. So, the company borrows, inflows will eventually come, everything will be fine with business, loans are not as frightening as we often think.

Another mistake I made from the start is targeting the customer but also the price range of my products. One thing I learned from practicing law is that it's always wiser to value your work more. Ray-Ban glasses, in production, can be bought for 5 euros, as much as the cheapest set of sunglasses on the street, but the brand sells them for 600 euros. Why is this possible? First condition is that the brand targets a specific population that has more money, and the second condition is never to devalue your product. This means that the future of your brand depends on the first price at which you will sell your product. Someone will say, I get glasses for 5 euros, I'll make 5 times more, sell them for 25 euros. Yet, someone even more successful in business will say, I will sell the same glasses for 600 euros to a smaller number of people; I won't have too many logistics costs, fewer employees, less time to work, more time for myself. You'll say, you can't sell every product at high price, but that's the mistake. Recently, a social experiment was conducted. A group of people wanted to see consumer behavior when offered clothing they bought for a few dollars at prices of several hundred and thousand dollars, all under a fictional brand, elegantly equipping the store and selling this clothing as exclusive. All this was marketing-wise followed, so on the opening day of the store, hundreds of buyers flocked to buy this "expensive" clothing. When asking buyers if they were satisfied with the quality and design of the clothes, they had only words of praise, not sparing a dollar to buy such exclusive clothing. Human mentality is like that, and we must understand it to be successful businessmen. Money is a measure of success, but inversely, the price is a mark of quality and value. The more you charge someone for a product or service, the more they will appreciate that product or service, even if subconsciously they somehow understand that it's not worth that price; they will always find a way to justify their choice.

Eventually, they will say it's because of some external factor. As a lawyer, anyone I did a favor to, charged less, or worked for free, didn't appreciate my work even 1% as much as someone who paid the full price for services. Actually, this often backfired on me because understanding that my services are free, these clients often don't hesitate to constantly call, have meetings, and pressure me to do something that simply isn't possible to do within certain deadlines. In contrast, everyone I charged the full price always showed a higher level of understanding for my time, and even when they don't succeed in specific representation, they always find external reasons for failure. Of course, the legal profession is such that sometimes the best possible legal services that can be provided do not bear fruit, after all, there are always at least two sides in a dispute, one must lose.

The last mistake I made is personally managing the company. We lawyers have a saying, "A lawyer who represents himself has a fool for a client." This saying can be applied to every business. Never allow your personal opinions and feelings to prevail in managing your company; it's best, if possible, to leave such things to a third party with experience in business. This is precisely why wealthy people are less likely to start companies but first and foremost invest in people in other companies. Of course, the problem with that is that you can't invest a large amount of money if you start from scratch, and that's why earning that first money is the most difficult.

"Men and Women"

A painful topic for all men, judging by women, is marriage and starting a family. This is absolutely untrue, and I say this for a simple reason – marriage is exclusively a woman's need, and if a woman wants marriage from her man, she can always get it. To avoid sounding harsh, it's not that men hate marriage or the function of marriage; they simply don't feel the need to pursue it. A man's inherent behavior towards his female, whether married or not, remains the same – protector, provider, all aimed at reproduction at a fundamental level; everything else is a personality construct, and finer aspects dictate the alignment of characters, attitudes, and ideals.

Discussing the basic level of personality, it is crucial to understand that men have everything they would have in marriage right now, and even more. Hence, from a logical standpoint, marriage is not desirable. Historically, society found ways to preserve marriage as an institution, all with a common goal – to prevent children resulting from the union of a man and a woman from becoming a burden to society. Therefore, it was necessary for a woman to be a virgin, and this custom became a highly moral norm, even checked during the first night of marriage by the relatives in some states. There are many reasons why a virgin woman was considered preferable; the primary reason was to prevent unwanted pregnancies when there were no condoms or contraceptive methods, making every encounter extremely risky.

Furthermore, what if an unwanted pregnancy did occur? Society established moral and religious principles against abandoning the child, against infanticide, and also introduced the principle of revenge for the tarnished honor of the girl, marriage under threat, etc. All of this was done to take responsibility for one's offspring and shift the burden from society to the family. Modern times offer modern but also immoral solutions to this problem. Now it's possible to live without marriage, raise a family without a partner, enter a marriage with "stained morality," or undergo an abortion. Sometimes, it even seems desirable for a woman to have multiple partners, with virgins almost non-existent, and it becomes a modern competition of who has had more partners.

On the other hand, changing sexual partners leads to the emergence of sexually transmitted diseases. Today, medicine can cure almost all diseases, and even HIV, once a feared threat leading to death, has been reduced to a chronic illness. Having multiple sexual partners also leads to confusion regarding who fertilized the egg. Nowadays, even this issue is resolvable.

Despite all of the above, there is one question that modern science cannot solve – the psychological impact of promiscuity. The psychological impact can be twofold: from the man's perspective towards a promiscuous woman and the psychological self-impact of a large number of partners on a promiscuous woman.

Men have an inherent understanding of a woman's modesty, innocence, and integrity. A man is inherently rougher. A man is someone who will "lead" a woman, take care of her and their children, and, on the other hand, the more innocent a woman, the better the chances of survival for this union. According to the assumption, a gentle woman is a better mother, a better wife. A gentle woman will take care of the home, avoiding conflicts. The daily life of a man in the 19th century, for example, is not at all that easy. For him to come home, clean, cook, change diapers, and, when he wants to be close to his wife, be rejected sexually, to go to work after a fight and return home in silence was unacceptable. Unfortunately, most of this has now become the standard for a man, so it's not surprising that a man's nature leads him to choose partners who meet these criteria.

From a man's point of view, a promiscuous woman is a naturally bad choice for starting a family. In addition, it is a man's nature to provide his partner with certain experiences. Thus, a woman will always remember her first sexual partner, even if the relationship was mildly terrible, and men are aware of this. Although we may not show it because it is a minimal part of all the problems that life can throw at us, every man can be asked whether he would prefer his wife to have been a virgin before marriage, and each would answer affirmatively. Society tries to suppress this natural behavior and understanding of a man as something archaic, all in the name of establishing a new normal, but nature cannot be suppressed. The same problem arises in marriages where a woman grew up in a wealthy family and married a poor man. Although on a daily basis, the man may not have significant difficulties functioning with a wealthy wife, but there will always be a dark part of the soul that regrets not providing it to her. How to impress someone, achieve goals, enjoy with it, progress both as a person and professionally, with someone accustomed to that standard. The man aims to impress his partner like a peacock and is chosen based on those impressions on the female gender. Sometimes it's physical appearance, sometimes money, sometimes success, emotional intelligence, etc. Of course, every man thinks he is the most beautiful, the most handsome, the most capable, the best man his partner has ever met because if he wasn't, she would surely find someone better. Joking aside, this is true.

Why does a man "suffer" from the need to be the best? The answer lies in our nature. We conquer women; they choose us. So, it's up to us to create an impression of our value, to show why marriage with us would create progress and healthy offspring. This reason is one of the reasons why women and men look at sex differently. Sex is proof of a man's worth! Sex is respect! For women, sex is not that profoundly ego oriented. Therefore, a man even tries to bring his partner to enjoyment and climax in sex, seeing the opposite as a defeat of his masculinity. Even in sex that he loves so much, as women rightly notice, a man fights another battle to present himself as a superior partner who will provide the best satisfaction to his wife. Women are not concerned about their sexual partner when it comes to sex unless it is meaningful because they love their man and want to give him the pleasure both deserves. The women are always a priority for the man in sex, by nature. Even the most selfish man in the world will react the same as the most selfless one because a man measures his success based on his partner's satisfaction.

A promiscuous woman is emotionally less sensitive to certain emotions related to her first partner; the first sex with the first and twentieth partner is not the same excitement, even though the twentieth is undoubtedly much better. Yes, she will have a "healthier" human relationship with the partner she lives with, but far less emotional. A man's success in bed when the goal is to prove himself as a worthy partner is her normal and expected because she has changed dozens of partners, and probably felt more significant sexual satisfaction with someone, certainly much greater emotions with the first partner.

Many women will say men can't stand strong women; that they don't have what it takes to deal with them. They will say the sexual experiences they had are positive because she knows how to satisfy a man, and so on. All this is a simple degeneration from the male view of a natural woman's modesty. Being a strong woman and presenting oneself as something to fight against, not to love and admire, is the first thing that repels men. A man, as a self-sufficient fighter for his bright future and offspring, doesn't need a woman to fight with but one with whom he will achieve his bright future. On the other hand, the fact that a woman knows and/or has done some things in bed that her man hasn't, and in which, of course, he is not the best in the world, will repel a man. From a male point of view, it is more acceptable for a woman not to have done anything with anyone because, surely, such a woman will have all the most beautiful experiences with him, and most importantly, they will participate in it together. For the same reason, no normal man would marry a porn actress. Setting aside morality and society's often hypocritical condemnation, at the most basic level, a man would always prefer a moderately beautiful virgin to the best and most beautiful porn actress. With the first, he can be the man he thinks he is, but not with the second.

From the perspective of promiscuity, a man's attitude is somewhat hypocritical, but it has its explanation based on the aforementioned principles. Therefore, a man seeks a woman with as few partners as possible, but at the same time, it is desirable in society that he himself has as many partners as possible. Simple math, which speaks in favor of a 50/50 ratio between men and women, tells us that these attitudes are diametrically opposed and impossible. However, the number of sexual partners has a completely different psychological meaning for a man than it does for women. A man is a conqueror, as we hinted earlier. Starting from the premise of what kind of conqueror he is when he has not conquered any woman so far, we quickly come to the answer that promiscuity in men is actually desirable. Of course, from a female point of view, until the moment a man meets her, a man who can conquer many women is immediately desirable, which is absolutely logical because if he could conquer all those women, then his value as a partner is great. At the basic level, such a man is a desirable partner for reproduction.

Women quickly test every man who tries to conquer them, even if they often do so unconsciously. Women set a series of tests for men to show their masculinity and quality to become their partner. Here, we come to an unnatural state. Namely, a promiscuous woman, not just a promiscuous one, but today's trend of women that Hollywood persistently tries to present as something normal and desirable, that is, more and more women seeking only sex, easy entertainment without attachment, consistently choose the same type of men and favor the wrong selection instead of natural selection. Then we come to a situation where the standards that women should set are completely lost, creating an unnatural situation where some less worthy men get easy "fun," or rather, easily get sex, not in a naturally traditional way. Then, seeing that this is possible, other men unconsciously try to gain sexual partners in the same way. How many times has it happened to us to go out just "to pick up someone," as teenagers say? Some locations become a desirable place for unworthy men to find easy women. It no longer matters what they have to offer to each other; the music is too loud, inhibitions are dulled by alcohol...

The problem arises when a woman, after this period of wrong choices in men, yet driven by nature because her biological clock is ticking, tries to find a suitable partner. Her experience tells her where to find them; on the other hand, the experience of such partners tells them where to find easy women because their goal is not a family. Therefore, women and men accustomed to degenerative behavior and frequent engagement in sexual relationships often fall into the vicious circle of repeated wrong choices, as all previous experiences have been bad. We often hear "you're all the same" and even worse, "all women are whores."

Absolutely not wanting to sound hypocritical, we should ask these men and women why they didn't meet in church but in a nightclub? Normal women and normal men are all around you – on the way to work, at the workplace, in the supermarket, on the street, in church, everywhere. The problem is that they are invisible. The more visible and more desirable,will be someone you know has had more partners, than a random man on the street, even though he may be a much better choice. You, as a stoic man, should not run away from nature; it is normal in a way, but at the same time, you should not engage in degenerative behaviors that are against nature and reduce a person's value and morality.

"Entering Marriage, a Value test"

Why is marriage necessary then? Without delving into an attempt to explain why marriage is necessary for women, I will try to explain the perspective of marriage from the male point of view.

The reasons why men enter the marriage are as follows:

- Religious and traditional
- Status-related
- Economic
- Emotional
- Wrong reasons

Firstly, religious and traditional reasons, especially, play a significant role in our society. Since a young age, we acquire a moral compass that marriage is desirable, good, a kind of life goal, and something that simply must be done. Religious reasons for maintaining the sanctity of marriage have already been explained earlier; religion, like any ideology, is devised by society to serve a specific social purpose, which I will elaborate on later.

The status-related reason is perhaps the most crucial for a man. As explained earlier, a man "suffers" from the need to present himself as an exceptional man, a gentleman, a respected member of society. When a man has a wife, children, a good job, a house, and friends, he then has everything from the society's point of view. Such a man is automatically of higher quality than other men in society who lack some of these elements. When a man has a quality wife, preferably educated, who has given him children, he is also considered high-quality because, if not, he would not have been successful in seducing, marrying, and having offspring with her. His wife is his status; his happiness in marriage is his reputation; his well-behaved children are his honor. Status, therefore, is crucial when it comes to the question of marriage. A man cannot be a fulfilled man if he does not fulfill himself through his offspring. Offspring is an opportunity for the good word about his successes to spread to other generations—his children, grandchildren, and great-grandchildren. Likewise, a man is obligated to his ancestors to be worthy of their sacrifice and their names.

A good wife is the building block for a man's development. Someone who will either support him to progress or be a stumbling block. A man is proud of his wife; she is a reflection of himself. It may sound a bit harsh, but she is also his trophy, which in no way diminishes the emotional part of marriage and the love we can feel for our better halves.

Economic reasons for entering marriage are clear; it is easier to share the costs of living when both partners work and contribute jointly. It is easier to provide children with everything they desire. It is crucial for a man to provide his children with at least the minimum of what he had. When we look at our parents, we know they did their best to make their exceptional our normal.

This is a sentence that left a strong impression on me and made me look at myself as someone's child and, at the same time, understand the daily struggle of my parents, especially my father, whose struggles as a man I can now comprehend, especially in the time he lived and fought for every meal.

The moment we realize the meaning of this sentence, it is already too late to change some things, but as a lesson for future generations, we must speak to our children. "Children, everything that is normal for you was exceptional for your parents. All their struggle for you to live the way you do is part of their dream." The birth of a child is the beginning of another race and a new struggle. A struggle to provide the child with everything we dream of at the time when it truly needs it. This part, "at the time when it truly needs it," is perhaps the most challenging to achieve.

Emotional reasons for entering into marriage are, of course, important; however, from the standpoint of a normal man, there is no difference in emotional approach before and after entering into marriage. The desire to get married emotionally is more of a need to surprise the partner, to give her a dreamy wedding, to make her happy.

It is unlikely that a man will be happy about a party where he has to take pictures with the entire extended family hundreds of times while sweating in a suit with a tie. However, if that is something his partner has dreamed of for years, he will be the happiest man in the world to make it happen for her. This is precisely why the female element is essential in proposing. The woman is the one who initiates the proposal, not by saying "propose to me," but by sincerely showing that it would make her happy. It is wrong to create resentment because the man did not propose to you; some might do it if they succumb to pressure, but this is not an emotional reason. Show him that you would be happy because of it, and that is enough for him if he considers himself your man. If your man loves you, he will do it at your suggestion that you want to get married, and he will be happy to do it because it will make you happy!

For a man, the act itself means very little in most cases. We are much simpler and emotionally unintelligent beings. As I write this, I remember the last vacation with my wife without children while lying on the beach and laughing at the typical "dad" poses of poor men whom women obviously "dragged" on vacation. Middle-aged guys were standing in Speedo swimsuits on the beach, hands on hips, watching the sea, and checking "where the danger is coming from," the younger ones eat and drink and turn to look at attractive girls, and the youngest ones make some castles in the sand and dig holes on the beach. Hundreds of men on the beach, and we can all be divided into these three groups, and none of them is 100% happy to sit in the sun, while the ladies, of course, shine with emotions. Yes, that's how we are, somewhat disinterested in the beach, which does not mean that we won't jump on a shark if it attacks someone in the shallows to defend women and children on the beach. It is the same regarding marriage; indifference exists, but there is also a great desire to make a loved one happy.

We also come for the wrong reasons to enter marriage. The pinnacle of all the wrong reasons for entering marriage is regular sex. Simply put, that won't be the case, and I think all men somehow understand it but still hope for the opposite. After the conclusion of marriage, a period usually comes for raising a family, the strongest professional development, hormonal declines, and imbalances in both genders. These are all reasons, as well as, of course, a kind of saturation with each other, that sometimes regular intimacy is replaced by irregular, often planned, and without too much excitement. Of course, there is a remedy for this too. Regularly work on yourself and your marriage, make an effort to maintain your commitment to each other even when you are tired and saturated with life in general.

Another wrong reason is "catching" a man with the intention of "settling down." Primarily, a man's nature is to be a conqueror. Settling a man with any kind of "fishing" is contrary to nature. Therefore, that man will not have the impression that he has achieved anything and will seek satisfaction of his natural needs for further conquest elsewhere. This is often seen in wrong relationships that arise in a similar way as described earlier. Two immature individuals attempting to limit their immaturity through marriage only lead to them seeing marriage as a cage and a restriction of their own freedoms.

A less wrong reason, but still wrong in some way, is unwanted offspring. A less wrong reason is that after some time, a man and a woman may actually establish a quality marriage by tying their allegiance to a common goal. However, there is always the possibility that this could be a dysfunctional family leading to divorce.

Prearranged marriages.

Prearranged marriages are only possible if the woman is physically and emotionally innocent. The reason for this is that any other combination would lead to the impossibility of the woman accepting the imposition of a partner who has not conquered her. On the other hand, a man will easily accept this option precisely because, at his basic human level, it represents a potentially ideal partner.

My personal experience of entering into marriage is what I would recommend to everyone. I met my wife and the love of my life at the moment when I had just finished college and found an internship. Somewhat lost in all the madness and life changes that accompany this period, unburdened by old relationships and somewhat tired of aimless dating. An idyllic meeting at a dance school, which, of course, neither of us completed because we replaced weekly training with better-spent time. However, it took 4 years until the proposal and 5 years until marriage, so after a full 5 years of dating. I always openly told my now-wife that I wanted her to finish college before proposing to her. I justified this to myself for two reasons: first, because of her, knowing that it would be very difficult for her to finish college burdened with children and obligations, and second, for status reasons. Perhaps a somewhat selfish reason, but looking from the extremely objective standpoint of a modern Homo sapiens, as a man who has a high opinion of himself and aspires to a bright future, I need a person who can keep up with that, good genetic material and a quality example for our children, as well as for us as a family of two intellectuals with high incomes.

My wife is strong, insightful, sometimes overly honest, a true Serb-Montenegrin with a firm stance and an incomparable skill of testing boundaries. I can freely say that I have grown into the man I am now from being in a relationship with her and conquering her was one of the most challenging love experiences I have ever had. Although unintentionally, it is about an innate instinct; all my masculinity, attitudes, principles, she put through countless tests. Strong, quality women do this. She will probably laugh reading the lines of this book because she often doesn't see herself as a strong woman. Her innate instinct woMAN.EXE; put me, a potential partner, to the test of values: am I good enough as a future father, as a future husband, as a sexual partner, am I desirable enough, can she trust that I will create enough money to feed our future family, provide us with everything we need and more, will her family love me, can I defend her in a physical altercation. All these are tests that every woman, when she meets a man, is obliged to conduct to be sure that she is allowing a worthy partner to create a community with her.

Men, of course, do not notice this because our matching test naturally ends somewhere at the width of the hips.

This is one of the reasons why girls often seek older men for dating. They are self-aware enough of their existence and easily overcome female tests through experience. There was a time when the entire range of these questions was unknown and temporally distant to me, so I simply didn't think that anyone would test me; 'Love me as I am, not as you want me to be,' I often said, and by this showing the entire spectrum of my immaturity.

A person's personality is not static; if they don't want to progress, then they simply aren't worthy enough. The dynamics of personality development show the quality of a man. The infamous desire of women to change a man is nothing more than a test to see if this man is capable of change, of progress. No woman actually wants to change a man into the ideal version of what she thinks a man should be because, very openly, women don't know what the ideal version of a man should be. They are guided by their own ideal version of themselves, and like in a mirror, they believe that their man should be like that too. On the other hand, a man should not accept change because he loses the essence that makes him a man, a leader of the pack. This is where many problems arise in male-female relationships;

women who give up seeing that the man is not changing at all or changing him so much that he ceases to be the person who attracted them. On the other hand, men who don't want to grow up or allow the woman to take on the role of the pack leader, losing everything.

Finding an ideal solution to this male-female problem is not possible. Each of us grows differently, but the safest solution from the man's point of view is to replace the changes that a woman demands by testing him with changes related to the development of his personality, profession, or body. Will successful business you made and money or regular training that will bring your body to perfection will replace, for example, long hair that has been your trademark for decades? Of course not, the problem of long hair will still exist, but you will unconsciously 'pass the test' of the possibility of change and development. Of course, if you don't want to change your image as a thirty-five-year-old rocker, then at least be a successful businessman, a quality father, always a desirable guest in the family, etc.

Taking boyfriend to meet the family also serves as a big test. No matter what your partner's family is like, no matter what personal opinion you have of them, they are the closest people she has had for decades, and you owe them respect. This also applies in the opposite direction towards the members of your family by the partner. They are, or some of them are, people she confided in during the toughest moments, parents who raised her from 3.5 kilograms, brothers who got beaten defending her from others, sisters who hid that she secretly went out to meet that not-so-quality boyfriend. They are her world, and it is very important that she can incorporate you into her world because any other alternative leads to the loss of one of you. No matter how much she says it doesn't matter to her and that no one will determine who she dates, this is one of the most important tests for us men. It's almost as important as when she introduces you to her little niece of a year and a half, unconsciously waiting for the reaction of both sides, will she notice a fatherly instinct? You must show respect to them; a woman needs someone who will take care of her and her family. On the other hand, demand respect for your family, for your previous family, even if you have a completely justified negative opinion of them. This conflict is often the cause of breakups and divorces; I've divorced so many marriages in my career, and each had an element of conflict between the new family and the old one, whether it's a husband with the wife's parents or a wife with the husband's parents, with sisters, brothers; it's always this problem that simmers, sometimes as the cause but not the pretext for divorce. It is like taking bandage of; it might hurt for a moment, but you can also peel it off for years, but it will still hurt a lot. These boundaries are necessary for your partner too; she will unconsciously respect you for that, but she will also know that you are capable and have that "fight" in you to protect your family.

You cannot prepare or copy answers to women's tests; just be aware that they will be there, always, unexpectedly for both you and her. The only way to be sure that you have done the best you can is to be the best version of yourself. If it's a test of protection for your loved ones, you won't pass it by having 150 kilograms or being a featherweight; you'll pass it by trying to get your physical appearance in a state of constant readiness. Of course, you shouldn't carry knives, guns, or any kind of shortcut to raw physical strength. MAN.EXE and woMAN.EXE communicate on a nonverbal, unconscious level, and a sense of security will not be created by dependence on weapons and tools, in fact, the opposite.

Masculinity is something that should not be under attack, even from your family, because your wife needs a man, father, husband, daddy for your kids who can be nothing else but a man. Set boundaries. It is very important to know what the boundaries are in every type of relationship, not just with a partner. Women are masters at testing a man's boundaries. Boundaries are desirable, boundaries are somewhat sexy, which is actually logical. Everything that is obtained with great effort is more desirable, it creates that feeling of success. A person's nature is to take everything they are given, but also to take everything as long as are given, and every time we give something without effort, that something becomes less valuable. In fact, the expectation is that we will give again next time. The same goes for boundaries; if we don't set them, they will be moved more and more to our detriment. Why do I say that women like to test a man's boundaries? Actually, it's in their nature. First and foremost, a woman tests a man's characteristics and determines if he is a suitable partner for reproduction. Since she cannot test his decisiveness and suitability by making a decision based solely on physical characteristics and practically seeing with her own eyes that he is a warrior and protector, she does so by attacking his integrity. The idea is that by testing a man's boundaries, she is trying to provoke the protector and soldier in him, to determine if he is capable of defending her or will run away at the first attack. When a man constantly yields to these attacks, showing that he has no integrity and no 'self,' even unconsciously, a woman sees him as a weakling. In translation, she imagines a situation in which an attacker kills them because her man does not want and cannot protect his boundaries. I'm not saying we should be unwavering in everything, but it is essential that we can assess when it comes to a test and when it comes to real mistakes we make. Imagine telling a child that they can eat one chocolate bar, and that is the limit. The child will eat the chocolate bar and be happy because they got a treat. However, if they ask for another, and you give them another, they will surely ask for a third, be very angry at the fourth because you refuse to give them another chocolate bar. Every time the child gets chocolate, they will ask for more and feel dissatisfied because they didn't get more chocolate as they are used to. The same goes for adults; a man's words and stance are only valuable when there are solid boundaries behind them that cannot be violated without consequences.

These boundaries need to be defended by any means, but at the same time, we must not allow boundaries to prevent us from achieving goals. Ego, stubbornness, vanity, or pride, as we call it, that feeling that hinders us from changing. A very toxic trait of every living being that arises as a product of testing a person's personal boundaries. Pride as stubbornness, pride as fear of others' opinions, pride as a belief that we are faultless, all these types are essentially limiting feelings for the development of human personality. I'm not saying we shouldn't have them at all, but we need to recognize when these feelings limit us in growth.

A goal big enough justifies any means, and pride particularly falls into that category. The famous writer Meša Selimović said, 'This feeling of pride is nice; it protects us from regret.' We use pride as a shield against bad decisions, and in the end, it hurts us a lot. Pride is a currency; pride should be used, when necessary, pay with pride when needed. A smart man doesn't allow someone's opinion and actions to influence him to the extent that he can make wrong decisions. Monetize the pride of others, play smart because at the end of the day, success is essential, not the way you achieved it.

The life of a man is a daily struggle, a fight for dominance, a fight for life, for success, for a partner. We, men, every day, even if we may not know it, are in a war, a war over everything we have and can have. To sleep through today and let loose, for me as a lawyer, means lost cases, means someone else will get that job, and true pride is not some falsely drawn lines of our imagination but that moment when we go to bed, at that moment, we should be satisfied with our success during the day; that's the pride we should strive for.

Ideals and principles are something everyone must have, but in the daily struggle with the whole world, they must be subordinated to the goal. Imagine if everyone in the world adhered to universal ideals and principles; it's only a matter of time before the first 'enlightened' man breaks them to defeat the others.

Often, when I talk and think about this, I remember the movie 'The Invention of Lying.' For those who haven't seen the movie, it's about an idyllic world where lying doesn't exist, until one moment when the first person lies and becomes the biggest and most famous face in the world, achieves wealth, the love of his life, etc. It's actually an incredibly good movie when it comes to the topic of MAN.EXE, the basic human program, and how twisting the reality of one man skews the reality of all others, and in the same moment, he becomes desirable despite obvious evolutionary and natural shortcomings.

"To every man upon this earth

Death cometh soon or late.

And how can man die better

Than facing fearful odds,

For the ashes of his fathers,

And the temples of his Gods."

Lays of Ancient Rome

What drives us in this battle with other men, with the whole world, to become ideal, the first and only leader of the pack of all men? First of all, let me distance myself from all those men who would say, "I just need a simple life, I don't want to rule, to be the best in every way." Look deep into yourselves, find the moment when you stopped believing in yourselves, when you stopped striving for perfection and the top of the pyramid, find the reason for that, and fight to revive once more that person who had dreams that defy gods – only you can awaken them again, take up the sword and shield, and return to the fight because that is our nature as men. I often hear pathetic statements like only women, children, and dogs are loved unconditionally, not men. That may be true, but it's not at all bad; it gives us the opportunity and obligation to always bring ourselves to perfection, something women, children, and dogs don't have to be. What is the success of someone who is loved unconditionally? What is the pleasure in success without a struggle, without sweat and sacrifice? There is no satisfaction, or if there is, it's short-lived, insignificant, and the enjoyment of it is minimal. Embrace the fact that you will be loved if you deserve it, but hold yourself accountable for merits, not others, and that is the source of true satisfaction.

Being happy is also something I avoid using. Children are happy when they get a toy (for 5 minutes). Happiness is category of feelings so often used, which we rarely experience any. If you asked someone on the street if they were happy, they would probably reason that they are, but does happiness even exist? Are we using it wrong in everyday use? I believe that a human being and a man, in general, should not use this term to describe the satisfaction and pride of success in life. Happiness is a very short-lived reaction to a situation or sensory satisfaction, and that is how we should perceive it, not subordinating the purpose of life to some imaginary happiness that essentially encompasses both success and pride, and various life satisfactions, family, health, work... A man has no right to mourn for happiness but to strive to be the best version of himself, and as such, he can achieve anything.

Life with a partner can be tough; you will have problems, conflicts, and occasional loss of interest in each other. There is no magic pill that can protect you from deceit, from suffering. My only advice is to stay true to yourself, believe in yourself and your masculinity, set boundaries because they are necessary to establish your legitimacy as a man, and most importantly, never rule out the possibility that you can leave. This power to leave gives you all the necessary strength in toxic relationships with a partner. Don't shy away from this possibility out of fear that you won't find better, that you'll be hurt, that you'll be alone. Being alone is not scary; it's the natural state of a man as a male, as an animal, which we are. Also, remember that the greatest successes are born out of the greatest sufferings, discomfort is good, and it is a prerequisite for development.

"Man and Fidelity"

The holy grail of women's fears. Man, and fidelity, can we even talk about it in one sentence when everyone knows that we are "pigs cheating on poor women"? There are so many misconceptions when it comes to male infidelity, endless quarrels, frayed nerves over something so easily solvable.

But let's start from the beginning. The female observation of a man and his qualities goes beyond objective evaluation points. Female observation and assessment of a man also go beyond subjective feelings. How many times do we hear from women, friends, sisters, girlfriends, "everything looks great, he's good, I like him, BUT he lacks that 'something.' Ah, that something, that drop of evil from the largest cauldrons of hell, the grain of sin, doubt, lust, all mixed by the devil himself... That seed of evil, so necessary, and yet so dangerous. That grain of passion that awakens doubts, fears, and anxieties, and without which life is simply boring. That imperfect, primordial element without which life is inconceivable because princesses cannot imagine a prince without a white horse not so much because they need the virtues and qualities of a prince, but also that dose of wildness that represents the horse. The prince on a white horse is a symbiosis. A magnificent Lipizzaner with a touch of untamed, born black only to become divinely white in a moment, refined, groomed. But is the soul still black or has it also polished over time? Yes, girls love the "horse." Quite logical. Now, imagine a Homo sapiens, sitting in his cave, all good, beautiful, offering love and attention, not ready to "fight" because he is too good. On the other hand, we have another primitive man, strong, with a scar from a fight with animals, not very cuddly, but capable of giving strong offspring, taking care of food, and not fearing wild animals and other men. The choice for this primitive woman is quite simple. The fact that he will give her strong offspring means a lot from the standpoint of choice. It's hard to understand this in today's world, but just a few hundred years ago, families and husbands themselves, in the event that a woman couldn't conceive with her husband, led her to have relations with a "trusted" man just to have offspring. Offspring was essential, incomprehensible in today's age. Healthy children meant not only the continuation of the name but also an "investment" in the future. There were no social systems, pensions, nursing homes, and methods of survival for the elderly and the sick independently of the family itself. You had to have a son, and not just any son but a strong, healthy one. In fact, you had to have at least five children because the chances that one of them would reach your old age were equal to the chances that you would reach old age, or very low. Mothers were in an even greater predicament; naturally, they lived longer than men did, engaged in less dangerous work, did not go to war. Consequently, the question of offspring was not a question but a necessity because that son had to support them in old age.

Now, considering these facts, would any Homo sapiens woman, for example, 10,000 years ago, risk her life, offspring, and old age for an incapable husband? Of course not. This is the basic instinct of finding a partner, not the most beautiful and kind, but the best option. So, women naturally need that "little wildness" to know that you will fight for her, to know that you will prioritize her and in future made the same offspring. However, such partners are logically sought not by one woman alone. This is where confusion arises when all of this is projected onto modern times. Women instinctively want what other women consider valuable. Nature usually ensures that this is true, but the needs of 10 centuries before Christ and the needs of the 21st century after Christ are not the same. Sacrificing a possibly more quality, beautiful life, equally quality offspring, all for the sake of a grain of wildness that will create more problems than benefits at any point in life, is a woman's greatest curse.

When a woman tests a man's fidelity, very often she does it not because of what he has done. It is interesting that a woman generally believes that her man will not cheat on her, but she does not trust other women not to try to seduce her man. This logic makes male-female relationships complicated and completely incomprehensible to men who unfortunately find themselves in a situation where he has to explain why imaginary women have no need to desire him, and at the same time present himself as desirable to his woman because if no one wants him, what's the point?

The plot twist is that the possibility of cheating is desirable and necessary. Of course, if cheating never happens, if it is, women hatred towards men transcends all laws of physics and logic. Even today, when you ask your partner, friend, sister about her past relationships, what do you think she will talk about, of course, the one where she was most hurt, but what she will never admit is that she would do the same all over again. She will not even remember the good guy who adored her; it's a paradox, a real paradox that simply forces men in the 21st century to adapt to these "insane" choices of women.

I'm exaggerating a bit, but the women need for a man to be untamed and slightly unfaithful is in the same league as if all men were looking for women with wider hips because only women with wider hips can carry a full pregnancy. Archaic and wrong, but natural in some sense.

The answer to the question of whether men cheat at all and whether it is inherent to them depends on the moment in a man's development. First, the basic instinct of a man deeply embedded in the MAN.EXE file is the instinct for reproduction, i.e., procreation. Logically, the goal of every man, somewhere viewed, would be to "plant seed" wherever possible. However, there is an evolutionary progress compared to animals. A much greater and more valuable instinct is parenthood and family support. These two instincts are conflicting because the moment a man has a child, he is no longer someone with the need for reproduction but becomes a father. As a father, his basic life goal is his children and family. If a man were to have more children with different women, then he would be forced to share time, food, and provide another accommodation with each family. Then these two goals become conflicting, and the more important one prevails, which is preserving the family and providing for the children. So, fundamentally, it seems like a man is naturally promiscuous, but even on that basic MAN.EXE program, it is not natural. A man will always choose to stay in the family and take care of and provide for the children, even if there is no love, sex, or any normal relationship with the spouse. This is a fact, and it has been proven many times, even seen many times in my profession. This fact allows, for example, alimony as a method of ensuring offspring in case of divorce. If men had no need to take care of their children, there is no law or force that would make them pay alimony to someone or be faithful for a moment, but that is not the case. Men are generally faithful.

Then, when is cheating "justified"? Although I can never sincerely justify it, the fact that someone is attached to you and has feelings for you obliges you to take care of those feelings. If there are some needs on the other side of a sexual nature, there are two solutions: first, improve the current sexual life, talk to your partner, work on passion, and the second solution, separate and look for another partner. Actually, the second option from a male point of view is not of a sexual nature, and I'm sure every man will confirm that. In 99.9% of cases, a man will not end a relationship because he needs more sex on the other side but because he lacks respect in the current relationship and does not feel the way he should, as a real man! So even though the opinion that men are only interested in sex prevails, it is absolutely not true. If we were to prioritize, the list would probably be uniform for all men in this order:

- Family
- Respect
- Love
- Relationship status
- Sex

So, when there is no family, when a man is looking for another half, first of all, he will demand respect. Respect is a much broader concept to be easily explained; for some, it is recognition that they are doing everything necessary to be recognized as men. For example, a sentence upon returning from work "come to rest, my love, you must have worked hard," or just a hug, even the farewell when leaving the house will mean more than hundreds of hours of checking messages on social media, endless "territory marking," and distancing your man from any existing breathing woman. Giving importance to a man that he is a supplier, that he is respected in his home will sustain every relationship better than the best sex in the world.

Of course, respect for a 15-year-old boy and a 40-year-old man is not the same. Maybe it will be more important for the boy to be recognized for developing six-pack abs, for example, or to be told that you are proud of him because he passed all the exams, or just that he is handsome because women rarely tell men, no matter how they look, but the principle is the same. Praise whenever there is an opportunity for something a man has done through hard work or be supportive, a safe haven, someone who will make his life better, easier.

A man's life is a struggle, even if we don't see it at first glance, our brain is working non-stop for creating success. Why do men especially love sports, enthusiastically cheer, watch games, because they identify the successes of those unknown people with themselves? In our heads, we are both Jokic and LeBron and Messi. We will watch the game and then go out with friends for football and break ourselves to win in an insignificant match. Some will even break a leg, but we will do our best to win because we are men. That's why we need a safe haven, to neglect all the fights and sacrifices in the hands of our more beautiful half, who will appreciate those fights, no matter how silly they look because they are what makes us men.

Love is something beautiful. A man's love for a woman is unconditional. A man loves a woman more than his life, and there is no different kind of love for a woman. Simply, he loves every element of her being, every wrinkle, every extra kilogram, every flaw because he does not see her as another being with flaws but as a deity that cannot be ugly, unsightly, fat, or whatever women notice as flaws. A woman he loves is our safe haven, the softest pillow, the most beautiful smell we want to experience. A woman is not just a woman but a divine collection of sensory experiences that quite accidentally has a beautiful form in our women. Besides that, she is also pride, a status symbol. Although women generally do not like it when men talk about them in this context, I think it is completely wrong to avoid men thinking about them sometimes as trophies. Women are our greatest trophy, proof that we have succeeded in the game of life, that we, as men, have found the ideal partner, who, besides looking so good, smelling good, having the most wonderful smile in the world, also strides next to us, chosen only by me and no one else, gave me children and is so perfect, so tidy that raises my reputation as an exceptional man. This is the feeling when we talk about a woman as a status symbol, but this feeling does not diminish the love we feel towards women, in fact, we love them more than ever, with a special sense of pride.

A man's love is the most wonderful thing that unfortunately women sometimes cannot understand. We are often misunderstood, marked as emotionally insensitive, and it is about two types of love. As I said earlier, a man shows his feeling of closeness through sex. We are not so good with words to show everything we feel, but if your man wants you, you can be completely sure of his fidelity.

Even if a man doesn't feel love, he often chooses to stay in a relationship simply because he is in a relationship. This is a strange situation that women cannot understand, but it can be easily explained by activating the "MAN.EXE" program. A man in a relationship has a purpose; he can give and raise offspring, build a family, and, of course, fulfill his sexual desires. Finally, there is also the possibility of falling in love, precisely from the sense of belonging and the potential for starting a family.

As a basic human being, a man doesn't prioritize a woman's individuality and intellectual qualities. He values her at higher levels of awareness, but fundamentally, respect comes first. Every man would prefer to create a family with a good and caring girl without much education, even if she's brought from the jungle, rather than with a doctorate holder who might love him but lacks respect or doesn't want a family. Education is just an accentuation in this example, and the reverse applies as well. The key is that if your man has respect and recognition for his abilities, you have him for life, and he won't think of another woman, no matter what you think about them (other girls), are they smarter prettier or whatever.

Male infidelity often stems from depression, from seeking light in a feeling of insignificance as a man. In such situations, a man tries to revive himself as a man, not necessarily to feel love but to feel masculine.

Women find it challenging to understand all this. I recall a conversation with my mother, a good and caring woman but lacking recognition of male needs. Throughout my life, I witnessed tensions in my parents' relationship. I often blamed my father for these conflicts, but as I grew older, I realized that neither of them was perfect. My mother gave birth to me at nineteen, while my father was 27, considerably older and just finished with his studies. Despite my mother's talents in painting and design, she never reached an academic level but that newer was an issue. The biggest problem she faced was not knowing how to use her femininity for her own benefit and for the sustainability of the relationship.

Especially, I observe that women who grew up with brothers tend to develop a more reserved side of character, unlike those raised with sisters. However, the real issue is my mother's failure to employ the reward principle, which men respond to so well. She often complained about my father not doing certain things, echoing common female grievances about men. We don't want to do what we're told. If we complained about women not doing what we told them, we'd probably be labeled male chauvinists. However, unlike women, there's a simple and wonderful method that women, for some reason, don't use. It's easier to get upset because we "forget" to do some chores around the house or because we went to the supermarket and bought beer and snacks but forgot shampoo "as if we don't need it". Instead, we should try to understand the male psyche and get everything you want while keeping a man who sees you as a goddess and doesn't think of cheating.

In short, whenever your man does something favorable to you, praise and be delighted, even if it's just an act of low importance. Or better yet, learn to appreciate it because it's not our obligation but goodwill (as a purebred man would say and, of course, be sanctioned like Yugoslavia for it).

Therefore, if you want your man to regularly mow the lawn and take care of the yard, the next time he starts mowing, bring a cold drink, interrupt him midway, and offer it because he's surely tired. Say, "You mowed wonderfully." If you want him to clean the bathroom more often, ask him, "Can you, when you find time, clean the bathroom thoroughly? I can't do it today." And, of course, enter at the end and say, "Wow, everything is shining" (even if it's not; it will shine next time). If you want your man to cook lunch more often, ask him, "What nice dish will you cook for me?" or "Will you cook something for me? I adore your food." Or "It turns me on when I see a man at the stove," and believe me, we'll be your pets, give our last breath of strength to please you because YOU APPRECIATE IT!

This is important because in my career, I see so many divorces and conflicts between husbands and wives based on stereotypes like "men don't do anything," "women nag." There is no physical barrier preventing a man from doing any of these things. In fact, the feeling of fulfillment and purpose will be a great reward over time when we achieve that sense. Physically, it's desirable to achieve PEACE at the end of the day by doing everything we can for our family so that these chores are not a reason for conflicts but require mutual understanding of differences. In fact, it requires a woman's understanding of a man because men are generally expected to take one more step beyond their nature-assigned functions.

In the past, a man supplied and fought against people and beasts. Today, there is no physical struggle; basic supplies—food, water, and shelter—are mostly there. So, there are no obstacles for men to get involved in household chores, taking care of children, especially if the woman also works and doesn't just fulfill her basic role in the family. I'm not saying this time and era is ideal; any loss of basic social functions leads to the collapse of society, as I mentioned in the example of mice. However, that doesn't mean we should blindly stick to our natural roles. We need to have balance in everything, to feel when replacing functions endangers the basic life function of a man because a man who doesn't perform his basic life functions in line with "MAN.EXE" is not a man, and it's up to the woman to, if there's no strict division of labor, work on convincing the man that he's indeed the perfect man. Of course, some basic functions can be compensated for by others. For example, a man earns excellently, works three days a week, provides for the family, and the family lives a good life. Still, his wife also works six days a week, so he's forced to take care of the house. In this situation, it's enough for the wife to encourage him to do a good job, occasionally say, "Thank you for doing this," and his masculinity won't be questioned. In contrast to this situation, we have a scenario where a man doesn't work, has no job, the woman works and supports the family, and she believes that it doesn't need much rewarding because if she works, he should take care of the house. This situation is not inconceivable and objectively unnatural, inevitably leading to a loss of a sense of masculinity, depression, and perhaps even infidelity, on both sides.

"Man and His Mother"

I won't approach this question like many, glorifying the bond between mother and son. It is clear to every living being that a mother's love is irreplaceable. The connection between every living being and their mother, especially a man and his mother, is something pure and emotionally closest to the love for a spouse and children. Of course, these are three different loves that cannot be compared or measured against each other because they are significantly distinct. Despite this clarity, its distinct nature often isn't very clear to us men, and even to our partners and mothers.

The conflict at this level, among the most important people in our lives, is perhaps the biggest reason for divorces, especially in Serbia where extended family life is still a reality. I cannot speak about the female position in this conflict because I don't understand it, nor am I attempting to. However, the reality is that there is a more or less concealed conflict between a mother and a wife, which evidently has been ongoing for ages.

Historically, the position of a mother was far more superior than it is today. Daughter-in-laws were once in a very difficult position, starting from arranged marriages, underage pregnancies, to some historically unthinkable customs such as the burning of widows (Sati practice in India), the custom of the first wedding night, bizarre genital mutilations, etc.

Very often, this sadomasochism was transmitted from mother-in-law to daughter-in-law, from mother to daughter, within a cursed circle of enforcing respect for some bizarre customs. Surprisingly, historically, it was women who compelled new generations of women to respect sick traditions, not men! This behavior is paradoxical, and there is probably a psychological explanation that could unravel it, similar to the Stockholm Syndrome but modified to some extent.

Growing up in rural Serbia, I noticed that older women, particularly those in rural areas, are the ones desperately trying to uphold some old traditions. In the Balkan region where the Vlach ethnic group resides, we have customs like the Black Wedding, fortune-telling, prophecy, and similar practices. Generally, women are more prone to swing into the esoteric, believing in horoscopes, natal charts, numerology, and other superstitions. I believe this is connected to women's pronounced emotionality. Women have an innate need to attribute their emotional reactions to certain things and phenomena. Not just literally attributing the reaction but connecting with it on a spiritual level. Women need spiritual connection, and in the absence of a partner with whom they can connect, they associate themselves through interpretation in some astro-spiritual dimension.

In simple terms, men lack spirituality and emotional expression to provide satisfaction to women to an adequate extent. Men are stoics who base their judgments on reality and facts. In this lack of emotional satisfaction, women turn to other women, but also to superstition, providing an explanation for their behavior and reactions to some supernatural source, whether it's numbers, stars, birth dates, spells, magic, possession, or similar. Then, they equate themselves with this, taking superstition as a fact. This is precisely why they are more likely to pass on the same superstition to the next generations.

A man, as a practical being, wouldn't engage much in customs. The customs that men respect are generally related to religion (baptism, marriage, festivities) or involve sensory experiences, so they will respect all customs that result in the enjoyment of food and drink or customs related to social status.

Most of men's basic needs, according to MAN.EXE, can be counted on the fingers of one hand: the struggle for dominance over other men, food, reproduction, family protection, status, and legacy for future generations. Was it important for a man to prove his wife's innocence to the neighbors' and aunts? Certainly not. He probably fell asleep after that act, while the mother-in-law and aunts boasted with the stained sheets throughout the neighborhood.

The burden of customs and the need of mothers-in-law to impose them on their daughters-in-law, thereby subjugating them, have been maintained for centuries and have been the cause of conflicts. However, today, this cause is slowly dying, which is positive for the generations to come.

The second fundamental cause of conflict is love for the same man, son, or husband.

To us men, the difference between these two loves is completely clear, and we always try to weigh this conflict on the one hand out of respect for the woman who created and raised us, and on the other hand, for the woman we love, even though we often become guilty of the lack of reaction. Every divorce I have represented boiled down to this conflict, and the conflict between these two female figures is inevitable. The conflict between male halves is very rare, as well as the conflict between daughter-in-law and father-in-law, and it is usually reactive.

Why is this conflict a very painful point for men and leads to such severe consequences? The man is actually caught between two people he cares deeply about and doesn't understand why he is in that conflict himself because he is emotionally unintelligent and uninterested in conflict. For a man, the battle between his wife and mother over his love is incomprehensible because it's about two entirely different types of love that shouldn't be in conflict. In addition to being naturally lenient towards his chosen one, not only because he loves her but also because he simply lacks the emotional-verbal ability to fight against her, he is also lenient towards his mother, the only person who has supported him unconditionally since the day he was born.

The basic reason for a strong attachment to the mother is the absence of the father as a supportive and loving parent. Especially older generations had a very clear differentiation of male-female roles, where the father was the "firm hand" in the family. To be clear, this is not necessarily bad, but it is bad if the father has ONLY that role.

Throughout childhood and adolescence, a man actually has only one unconditional love, and that is the love of his mother. All other loves from the day of his birth until he becomes a father are with reservation, even future

112

wives. Love for a wife begins with a struggle, conquest, showing that we are worthy of her time, bed, and ultimately worthy of sharing a life together. And that "trial" never really ends; the consequences of a man's inadequacy are just less severe because after the birth of children, women find it much harder to decide to end the relationship.

This moment of the birth of a child creates confusion in family relationships. This is when a man grows up, realizes that his life is worth much less than the lives of his children, thus the inherent and natural love for his mother isn't as relevant to his life. It is replaced by the selfless, pure love of his children. Not only the love of the mother, but also the wife. Very often, problems in marriage arise at these moments, as the woman, accustomed to receiving unconditional love primarily from parents and then a partner, now shares that love with another being, even if it's her own child. It's not easy for her to know that she will be in second place.

Mothers simply must understand, and in doing so, they also grow, that our love for them will never cease, but it is not necessary for us because, well, we are not even necessary to ourselves to value it so much.

This is an interesting question that I asked myself at one point. Before having children, I would have given my life for my wife, out of love for her and considering it chivalrous. Most men would risk their lives to save their wives, save someone else's child, and often even an animal in danger. It's just something we men do, whether entering a burning building, going into wet trenches to defend our loved ones, always saying "women and children first." That's us, men, it's ingrained in our basic male code MAN.EXE. However, that moment comes when everything changes. The epilogue is somewhat similar, but the reasons are entirely different.

For example, even now, I would give my life for my wife, not because I love her so much that I couldn't live without her, but because I love my children to the extent that I couldn't allow them to lose their mother. For all other beings in danger, I would think very carefully before doing something that could jeopardize my life. This reaction is no longer automatic but calculated, as much as possible, if there is a chance, yes, if there is no chance, I won't sacrifice myself "because that's how it should be."

This is precisely why in the military and similar services, "young blood" is needed, not because young people are foolish enough not to appreciate their lives, but because their natural instincts don't allow them the possibility of thinking. The natural instinct of a young man tends toward competition, while an older man is geared towards defense and providing for the family, making the older more prone to surrender and risk avoidance, desertion.

A man grows up when he has his children but also when he realizes that there is no one who would be his "safe harbor" from life's hardships. When he realizes that there is no one to turn to except himself. When he becomes the one other turn to for help, a secure harbor for others. This moment, in all its grandeur, is also an immense stress and burden. I remember the first moments when I was in a situation to help my parents. On the one hand, I was happy that I could help them, and on the other, I felt such a heavy burden and anxiety because I finally understood that I am now the one who is the safe harbor, that my success is the success of my children, my mother, father, sister, and others who count on me. For this reason, I must always be ready to help, as I was once sure they would be there for me, no matter what happens.

This is a life struggle, a maturation that is by no means easy. Many would like to be able to curl up like they were as children, in their mother's lap, dreaming big dreams in a warm family home without worries and people who depend on us every day, hour, minute. Sometimes I think that not even half a minute passes without Tasa saying "dad" or Luka squatting down, offering his blanket for me to smell it (it's his thing). The sooner we get rid of this need and realize that we are that warm lap and secure harbor, that we are the support pillar, the machines for big dreams and selfless love, then we will grow into men as the creator programmed us, but we must never make the mistake that generations of men before us made. Be educators, be strict, but always tell your children that you love them, support them, don't allow only the mother to be the one providing unconditional love and support, and in doing so, you will give your children a gift for the future and create people full of love. Hug your children and tell them you love them, whether they are 5 days, 5 years, or 50. They are your children and will always be.

When I was little, 7-8 years old, my sister and I would always hug our mother before going to sleep, then hug our father and go to sleep. Due to frequent conflicts between my father and mother, one day I just decided not to hug him before going to sleep. It seems he didn't mind, so he didn't insist on it. To this day, I haven't hugged my father a second time, nor has he hugged me, even though we have a good relationship, even much better than before. That need for closeness somehow disappeared, but it is very necessary, and lately, I very often mentally break down, fearing that moment of emotional indifference with my own children.

Of course, keep in mind the fact that male and female children need to be raised differently. Make top-notch men out of your sons, prepare them for life, give them all the tools to be successful, but never deprive them of unconditional love, as many do, repeating generational trauma. Unloved individuals cannot love, at least not genuinely, often turning their feelings into love out of spite, creating unhealthy extremes. Thus, we have excessive love for the mother, repeating the pattern from childhood because the mother was the only one who provided love to the man, but also excessive love for their own children and an excessively protective attitude because in childhood, this person didn't receive enough love from one or both parents, so now they want to prove to themselves and others how to behave towards children. Every extreme creates unnatural feelings, stress, violent hacking of the MAN.EXE program, creating mentally unstable men and emotionally confused people in future generations who continue the wrong pattern of behavior, moving from one extreme to another."

And cherish the moments you have with your mothers, try to resolve problems like a man but keep in mind that you will always be a kid to her. Both of you will grow in time but life with and without a mother is incomparable. Few months ago, I discovered that she is suffering from cancer. The moments like this, and trauma like this will make you a very different person at the end but it's up to you what kind of person you will become, will it prevail anger and resentment or you will acknowledge that every moment spent with your family should be cherished and every chance to have a quality life should be taken. Its all up to you, it is hard, sometimes insufferable, but it is life, it's being a MAN.

"Struggle or to struggle"

Whether struggle or to struggle, is an eternal question of motivation. The problem is often described by the proverb "He who doesn't pay at the bridge will pay at the ferry," meaning that everything worth doing requires energy and involves discomfort. However, we often overlook the fact that the alternative also involves discomfort and struggle. Yes, it is difficult to train and be capable of defending oneself, but it is also challenging to stand up to bullies at school, run away or fight with an animal, win a physical fight, and eliminate threats, survive in a war... In reality, the alternatives are much worse, and if we add the inability to find a partner, extend the lineage, and establish a family, the meaning of existence is undermined. Life is a struggle, and that is a harsh fact. Instead of mourning it, let's take control of that struggle. It is better to consciously struggle than to allow life to test us unprepared. We can achieve this only if we mentally and physically prepare ourselves fully and strive for perfection.

I'm not saying that one should prepare for the worst because the worst will surely come. If we are lucky, we won't witness the death of a close family member, but we will certainly face our own mortality. We will be without money, and the majority of humanity is actually hungry and thirsty. We should live the best we can at this moment, give our all because it is blasphemous and contrary to all the principles of the generations that brought us into this world. We are here to continue their legacy, to live, but not just live; we should strive to live the best we can.

The chance that we were born is one in a billion, and being such an egoist that you know you won the lottery, yet take life for granted, is contrary to common sense, nature, God, and the lineage that brought us into the world among billions of possible gene combinations. A real man cares about the legacy he leaves for generations, whether he will be remembered, and his name recounted even after a hundred years.

My great-grandfather Vladimir, a participant in World War I, crossed Albania with the army, leaving his wife and six children at home. Upon his return from the war, five of his children died. All generational sufferings, and his were the most vivid, live within us. We need to ask ourselves if we have the decency to say that we find it difficult, that we can't fight, that we don't want a family because we can't support it. My great-grandfather for example, would have the right to slap me and say, "Did I give my life and the lives of my children for this? Is this wretch, just a few generations after my death, trampling on all the principles and values of our family name?" It is my duty as a man to justify all these sufferings, struggles, and sacrifices because our ancestors gave everything so that their exceptional becomes normal for us.

All the dreams and goals of our parents are our everyday reality, just as all our goals, successes, and dreams will be the new normal for our children. However, our children must know the sacrifices we, as generations, have made to achieve these goals. If they don't know, they won't feel the obligation of the family name to justify the expectations we have. They will become arrogant and ungrateful, thinking that it's the duty of others to give to them.

The role of a father is to instill this in the consciousness of his children, to pass on the stories of his ancestors, just as his father and grandfather told him. It is your sacred duty to make your child know where they come from, who their ancestors are, and to speak about everyone, their struggle, life. This way, they will develop a sense of belonging, primarily to the family. Today, this is one of the family's biggest tasks at a time when the system is slowly pushing for the dissolution of the family as the basic unit of society with cheap substitutes. When you instill a sense of belonging to the family in a child, they won't feel alone in the world and seek a replacement for the basic social cell. They won't feel the need to identify with other groups, to be like the EMOs or rockers in the past, and today, vegans, liberals, change genders, join fan groups, gangs, and so on.

Although I will probably be criticized for the last sentence, I will try to explain my position. When a person, in their growing up, childhood, and adolescence, has a clear sense of belonging to the family, cherishes the spirit of ancestors, the last name, and has someone to turn to whenever necessary, there is no need for artificial "finding oneself." They won't create needs for belonging to a group.

I sincerely believe that today's society is highly fragmented precisely because of the lack of a sense of belonging to the family. A child growing up in such a society tries to find their place in a group of people, and even unconsciously seeks the family elsewhere. Unfortunately, there are many cheap substitutes. Many may disagree with me and criticize me for this, but I believe that a significant number of today's vegans, gender dysphoric individuals, liberals/conservatives are actually young people who are lost in a world without a strong family connection. I'm not saying that gender dysphoria doesn't exist, but I can easily recognize when something is a trend and when it's a mental illness. 3% of all teenagers in New York are transgender. This means that roughly every 30th teenager is trans. On the other hand, research from a few years ago states that gender dysphoria affects one in 30,000 people. On the other hand, the LGBTQ community doesn't help much, it seems to me as an outsider interested in all social issues, including this one, that very often, as an alternative to identifying with one of the new genders, they offer suicide as a shadow that haunts all those who cannot find themselves. Hence, every year, we get a new letter in the LGBTQ acronym.

As someone with a gay person in the family, I cannot say that I am tainted with hatred or any prejudice on this issue; sexual orientation is a personal matter. The only thing that genuinely bothers me is the fact that for many members of "this community," sexual orientation represents personal identification for everything they do.

121

When asked, "Who are you?" the usual answer is the name, then the surname, then sexual orientation, and then profession, etc. When I ask myself the same question, I get the answer: name, surname, father of two children, husband, profession, etc. We get a similar answer from vegans, passionate football fans of a particular sports team, for example. The pride with which sexual orientation, belonging to a fan group, or choice of food is given importance, and the position of the family is evidence that many are seeking belonging due to the lack of a family, lack of a fatherly figure, and lack of family spirit. I personally don't have the need to identify with a group of people who eat plants or only meat, and to make it a "significant thing" in life. What would my great-grandfather Vladimir say? I would probably get a slap and the answer, "Where are my grandchildren? Did I fight with the Bulgarians and cross Albania for this?"

Jokes aside, the family is the one that provides primary experiences about different personality types, about good and bad. There's Uncle Jon, the alcoholic, don't be like him; be like Uncle Edvard, three children, a good job, loves his wife, a wonderful family, shining with prosperity, radiating warmth. Then, at celebrations, you hear about how great-grandfather Vladimir crossed Albania, how great-grandfather Gvozden baked bricks and built this house just three days before the start of World War II and the bombing of Belgrade, and it still stands firm, how they hid Grandma, then barely a teenager, in the basement from the "liberating" Russians, how he spent his whole life fighting against the communists who moved teachers from the elementary school into the house, intentionally used the toilet in the bucket whenever Grandpa and Grandma had lunch. But also, beautiful things, like how Grandpa married the most beautiful woman in the area, how he traveled to the neighboring village on a sleigh tied to horses for a saint's day celebration, how he never spoke a single bad word to Grandma in his entire life and remained faithful to her until his last breath. Then, my father, who smuggled laundry detergent, went to war, sold peppers from a truck without brakes, smuggled walnuts from Romania with Grandma and his uncle, somehow found the strength in his later years to become a lawyer, quit smoking even though he smoked four packs a day, all for the family celebration, while there is the burning candle, and the icon of the family saint who seems to watch over all of us and protect us from evil. So much wisdom, experience, blood, tears, and joy in these few stories, stories I've heard so many times that I've memorized them by heart, but stories I will gladly pass on to my children. These are experiences that build a child's personality, create awareness of the past, a sense of belonging, of good and evil, and the need to see both good and bad and know how to distinguish between the two.

For example, something that has stayed with me is the story of the army's retreat through Albania, what was called the Serbian Golgotha, and it definitely was, but in every evil, there is also good, and vice versa. We need to know that we as a nation are not without fault, so we know that Serbs suffered great sacrifices in this retreat, especially being attacked by Albanians, Serbia lost 60% of its population in First world war. However, few talk about the fact that when our army returned over Kosovo after breaking through the front, they often indiscriminately killed Albanians. Great-grandfather used to say how his unit passed through Kosovo and villages, and some soldiers would take bombs, and in the middle of the night, while Albanians were sleeping next to the fireplace with their families, they would throw a bomb through the window and wipe out entire villages.

The balance of good and bad is crucial, which we build for ourselves but also for our children. There is no good without bad, and no bad without good, because how would we know what is good if we didn't know how bad it is, and vice versa? When I think about the struggle of good and evil, I always remember the Native American proverb about the white and black wolves that we always have within us:

"A Cherokee elder is talking to his grandson about life. 'A battle is raging inside me,' he says. 'It is a terrible fight between two wolves. One is evil. It is anger, envy, sorrow, regret, arrogance, self-pity, guilt, resentment, lies, superiority, and ego.' He continued: 'The other is good. It is joy, peace, love, hope, serenity, humility, kindness, empathy, generosity, truth, and faith. The same fight is going on inside you and inside all other people.' The grandson thought about his grandfather's

124

words for a moment and asked, 'Which wolf will win?' The old Cherokee laughed and replied: 'Whichever one you feed.' The story continues. 'You see, if I only feed the white wolf, the black wolf will hide in the dark, waiting for me to stumble so he can attack and attract attention, which he craves. He will always be angry and always fight against the white wolf. But if I accept his existence, both he and the white wolf can be satisfied, and we all win. Because the black wolf has qualities that I need and that the white wolf lacks: persistence, courage, fearlessness, willpower, and resourcefulness. The white wolf, on the other hand, provides compassion, care, heart, and the ability to appreciate the needs of others compared to mine. You see, both wolves need each other. Feeding only one and starving the other will eventually make both uncontrollable. Taking care of both allows them to serve you so you can do something bigger, something good with your time on Earth. Feed them both, and you will quiet their internal struggle for your attention. And when there is no battle inside, you can hear the voices of deeper knowledge that will guide you in choosing the right path in every circumstance. Peace, my son, is what we all must strive for in life. He who has peace within has everything. He who nurtures a storm in his heart and soul has nothing. The way you choose to deal with opposing forces within you will ultimately determine how you live.'

Peace. Peace must be one of man's basic aspirations. We must distinguish, though, peace from the other two extremes of all the wolves that put our values to the test.

The basic human desire for peace is much more than psychological and physical peace. Peace is that moment at the end of the day when you look back at the day and say to yourself, 'I did a good job.' When you look at your children in bed, peacefully sleeping with full stomachs, your wife in your embrace with a smile, exhausted with that good tiredness that speaks of being physically alive and still grasping and seizing life with all your might. That you were a good father, dad, husband, son, friend, business partner, businessman, man, human being, that you fed all the wolves within you, and you can peacefully go to sleep. In this peace and balance, we should end the day, just as we should start it by bringing ourselves into a state of imbalance and readiness for battle. This is the natural course of life that begins with a struggle, a child's cry, to end with peace and a retrospective of life. Just as we shouldn't lament all the missed dreams, wishes, and goals on our deathbed, we shouldn't go to sleep knowing that we haven't brought our day to perfection in every aspect of life. If we think like this every day and strive for perfection every day, we won't regret any missed opportunities even on our last day.

"Man and Religion"

In the freezing dawn, on St. John's Day, I put on a jacket, boots, and grab a bag traditionally carried to church for cutting the cake. I place a cake neatly wrapped in white ceremonial cloth, adorned with delicate embroidery of forest flowers, grape leaves, and wheat, a small bottle of black wine usually homemade Hamburg, thick wax candle made of pure beeswax, and hang it on my shoulder just like generations of my ancestors did. I set off to the village monastery for cutting the cake and the morning liturgy, resembling a pilgrim.

I don't consider myself an especially religious person; I view religion in my own way. I harbor no illusion that I can understand how the world was created, whether and how God created humans, and who God is, in essence. As a man, I see myself as someone who approaches every question with the intention of finding answers, and if the answer is impossible to find, I don't think it's worth wasting time in aimless theorizing. If God exists and created us all, giving us social and biological roles, I believe being godly means being true to oneself, not violating the natural laws on which we have existed for thousands of years.

On the other hand, religion, in my opinion, has an entirely different role. Originating from the foundations of class struggle and the fight for the liberation of people, I think it has been used as a universal means of controlling the masses. If you're a poor medieval peasant and the feudal lord takes huge taxes, you have no choice but to pay. Then you turn to religion because it's all you have left, justifying such a life by believing in the heavenly kingdom after death, while this evil feudal lord faces hell.

Most religions have been used by rulers to pacify their subjects in the name of God. The fact that the imperial crown is given by God, the royal one by the Pope, leads us to the understanding that rulers used religion for control. It's not surprising that today, in the 21st century, religion is losing importance in Western countries, remaining consistent only where control is still necessary due to social and economic differences (South America, the Middle East).

However, regardless of the sense of the existence or non-existence of God as a supreme being, religion is something crucial for every man. Religion provides a countless of basic principles of living that are actually universal principles without which society could not exist. The commandments, however banal they may seem, are the first laws of humanity, and their source lies in the nature of human relations. A God-fearing person is a good person, good for society, for their family, and for their children, to whom they will instill correct principles. Should one adhere completely to these principles? Of course not! The era is such that if the Bible, Quran, and other holy books were taken literally, they would not allow us to live a normal life. However, the basic principles contained in each of them are crucial.

Another reason for the necessity of religion is its role in preserving the family, preserving good customs, and developing a sense of belonging to the community. It is not necessary to go to church every week to instill a sense of religiosity in your children. Preserve religion in your family; from an early age, take your children to cut the "slava" cake, decorate the tree together on Christmas Eve, and dye eggs for Easter, even though it has absolutely nothing to do with Christianity. All these are wonderful moments to bring the family together, to retell those family stories, and to build character. The same applies to members of all other religions; respect holidays, whether it's Christmas, Eid, Hanukkah, or something else – these are all moments that firmly connect us and create a sense of belonging to the family.

"Survival Instinct"

Sometimes, I truly believe there is some higher power, a cosmic force that propels and cares for us just when we need it most. However, I think we are the ones who can invoke it. How many times have you found yourself in a seemingly hopeless situation, only for "something" to happen and change your circumstances? When you're broke, a business opportunity emerges, bringing in profits just in the nick of time. What a religious person might attribute to a higher power, God, karma, or something else, I see as a force we can consciously summon.

The search for God must begin within us. According to the Bible, God created man in his own image, giving him the means and knowledge to survive and prosper. Man is different from animals to the extent that his purpose goes beyond mere survival and the continuation of the species; it involves making progress. However, this progress, this step forward, often becomes the reason for man's downfall.

Animals take from nature only what is necessary for survival, while humans strive to take everything and subjugate nature to themselves. Animals eat to stave off hunger; humans eat even when not hungry. Animals engage in sexual relations for reproduction; humans do it for pleasure. One of humanity's greatest challenges is finding the balance in satisfying needs because what drives us initially is more animalistic than human.

"MAN.EXE," as the basic human program, operates at this basic level of fulfilling needs. What we can do in the search for "God" within ourselves and His assistance is to do it always, not just in times of desperation. This means that if we need more money, we shouldn't wait for a moment of despair for "something to happen." That moment of despair is when "MAN.EXE" kicks in at 100% power. Nothing happens by chance; we consciously seek money and success, urgently seeking solutions, and unconsciously shaping our thoughts and attitudes so that others react to us. It's not God or karma; it's us, both consciously and unconsciously, because we need it then for the satisfaction of basic needs.

Why not use this knowledge now to our advantage? Instead of creating mindsets that attract success from seemingly hopeless situations, we can make a conscious effort to summon "MAN.EXE" at any time. As individuals reflect society on the smallest possible scale, the family reflects it on a slightly larger scale, and the state and global society on the largest scale. In times of greatest challenges, there is the greatest progress.

Where does the impulse to bounce back stronger than ever, to overcome adversities, to deal with setbacks come from? It comes from our good old "MAN.EXE"! Since we are aware that this is not the work of a higher power but only our inner strength and knowing that in today's world it is not difficult to satisfy all life's needs, we can bring our awareness and spirit to a state where "MAN.EXE" is always running in the background, controlling the reality we live in and providing us with constant stimulus for development.

The basic way to do this is to trick our autonomous system into thinking that the organism is in a state of need to activate "MAN.EXE." Some of the methods have been mentioned earlier, such as bathing in cold water early in the morning, which has nothing to do with masochism but with adrenaline and instinctive survival reactions. Besides triggering instinctive survival reactions, this clears thoughts and initiates the burning of fat reserves because the body begins to use these reserves, thinking that survival is at stake. Skipping breakfast is not about starvation or losing weight but about putting the body in discomfort and preventing it from becoming overly satisfied, thus shutting down "MAN.EXE" and producing too many happiness hormones, which can mislead us into thinking everything is ideal.

In fact, we should always be a little hungry, always a little cold, a little uncomfortable because these are the things that activate innate survival reactions. Training is not just about achieving a goal but also about the journey because training and physical work, in general, are stressful moments for our bodies. The body fights against the effort on a psychological and physical level and retains a state of heightened attention for hours after the training. When you don't have a girlfriend and regular relationships, the worst thing you can do is seek cheap substitutes for it. Having friends for emotional support, watching porn for "release," engaging in online chats with girls for a false sense of dating – these are things that kill your every chance of satisfying your needs. Your body and thoughts must go hunting for a partner; you must be hungry and eager for it, not settling for cheap substitutes because every time you do, you kill your desire to find a partner, shut down "MAN.EXE," and prolong the situation.

Yes, you have to want everything very much to get it, to want success, money, love, sex. To be a hunter at every moment on that path. Don't deceive yourself into thinking that some higher power will fulfill your needs; everything you need lies within you. Instead of being victims of chance, be masters of yourselves, your bodies, and thoughts, and therefore, of reality. As I have already mentioned, reality exists within us; we create reality, so why not distort it to such an extent that it favors us? Never have a Plan B. Plan B is the worst thing you can do for your success. Your consciousness, attention, and goals must always be directed toward one goal. Having a Plan B means achieving Plan B. I never allow myself to have alternative goals; I don't want to think about them because, like a bad omen, they create insecurity.

Often, religious people say that God tests us to teach us to cope with life's difficulties. The well-known quote by an unknown author also reflects this sentiment.

I asked for strength

and God gave me difficulties to make me strong.

I asked for wisdom

and God gave me problems to learn to solve.

I asked for prosperity

and God gave me a brain and brawn to work.

I asked for courage

and God gave me dangers to overcome.

I asked for love

and God gave me people to help.

I asked for favours

and God gave me opportunities.

I received nothing I wanted.

I received everything I needed.

Whether it's God, another supreme being, karma, the universe, or ourselves, the lesson is the same: to overcome challenges, we must face them. How would we know what is good without experiencing the bad, or what is bad without feeling well-being?

There is no need to fear or avoid difficulties. In the final equation of your life, there will be larger and smaller difficulties to deal with. Every struggle with difficulties means that the ultimate result is more positive. Take it a step further, enjoy that battle because, just as every reward brings satisfaction, the feeling of success, the feeling that you have overcome hardships, creates a sense of satisfaction—often stronger and more lasting than some small pleasures. Create a dependency on this feeling, of small successes, larger ones, and the greatest ones that are least common. Every success, even the smallest, will make your body release happiness hormones as a reward.

When you see and perceive yourself as a highly successful person, self-satisfied because every day you create new victories, you will create the reality of yourself as a winner. This reality will naturally attract new successes, new people to collaborate with, and the pleasant feeling of your environment that will want to stay with you, absorbing the positive energy you radiate. As I mentioned, success is relative. What is considered success to someone—earning enough for a personal home, taking care of the family—might be different for another, who may only consider themselves successful after becoming a millionaire. Yet, be sure that the third person, not satisfied even with a billion, hasn't come close to a billion considering themselves a loser because they can't make a billion. You can be successful with just a hundred euros, but you must not stop there. Being successful implies longevity, repeating success, and raising the bar.

"Emotional Scars"

Do not fear emotional scars but strive to create them where necessary. Generally, like any discomfort, emotional scars are something we tend to avoid. Men, in particular, are less emotionally intelligent than women, who gladly utilize their empathy and emotional connection. We struggle in that regard. Men are problem solvers, and any form of emotional disturbance causes us stress. We avoid arguments with the other sex because every negativity truly hurts us and damages us on an emotional level. When I say not to be afraid of emotional scars, I don't mean you should argue and quarrel endlessly until you toughen up. On the contrary, choose your battles wisely.

Many years ago, I read a book called "Flinch" by Julian Smith. In short, it suggests breaking the insecurity and flinch we have—a subconscious body defense reaction. To exaggerate, if you need more self-confidence, go out on the street naked. You will never have self-confidence issues again because nothing can be as bad as the day you went out naked. Every emotional scar creates a subconscious body reaction similar to when your life is threatened, but you are aware that it is not that bad. For example, many men have an insurmountable fear of meeting people of the opposite sex. Although they might be very valuable, look great, and be successful in every sense of the word, they simply struggle to approach someone of the female gender. And when they overcome that fear, they can't say anything intelligent to leave a good first impression.

This fear is sometimes so intense that it paralyzes a man completely, similar to a deer caught in the headlights of a car. The basic feeling of life-threatening danger at the subconscious level, as much as it would be activated if their life were genuinely in danger, activates in these harmless situations. Pre-planned sentences, pickup lines, or anything else don't help. The same thing happens with some students. We've heard hundreds of times the phrase, "I studied everything, but when the professor called me, I froze and couldn't remember anything."

The reason for this, in my opinion, is biological. Some simply lack experience, or their organism does not differentiate the severity of the threat, so it releases the wrong set of hormones at the wrong time, creating the "deer in the headlights" effect. The good thing is that this inherent reflex can be corrected. It just requires deliberately creating as many emotional scars in that place as possible so that our body gets used to this feeling. For example, the remedy for a man who is afraid to approach a girl he likes is straightforward—talk to as many women as you don't know. You can start with an old lady at the market, the cashier, and say something banal like "have a nice day" or "can you return this chocolate, I changed my mind about buying it." Of course, this takes a bit longer. From personal experience, I think it's better to twice make a fool of yourself by nonchalantly approaching, leaving a terrible first impression. By the third time, you will probably not feel fear anymore. Don't worry; she will forget your bad approach because she probably won't see you again and be sure that you are likely at least the third one this week with a bad pickup line. We're not all Casanovas, nor are Casanovas born. Speaking of this, Thomas Edison said, "I have not failed. I've just found 10,000 ways that won't work."

You should also use emotional scars to your advantage. You don't have to be reactive and remember these words only when you lack something, when you can approach a girl, pass an exam, or succeed in a job interview. Be proactive, and deliberately create scars where you want to progress because these scars will make you better and stronger. As an attorney like me needs to be an excellent speaker, I consider myself pretty good in court, but if I want to be even better, I'll do something that creates discomfort for me. For example, I'll go to a stand-up comedy night and embarrass myself like never before. Once, twice—on the third attempt, I will probably have a decent performance. This "embarrassment" will bring me the skill of improvisation, and it will be useful in my further business. Consider which skill will benefit you, and then find a way to deliberately make yourself uncomfortable to target those deficiencies you have. From these scars, a better and stronger man will develop. Use this often, evolve. Sometimes this also works on a physical level; if you want to jump higher, do exercises that will develop those muscles. Similarly, on a psychological level, when you exercise, you create micro-damage to muscles. The muscle then heals and becomes stronger. MMA fighters, for example, intentionally injure their shins or wrists, and over time, those parts of the body harden and become stronger than before. Every strike, every micro-fracture, by healing, strengthens the bone, the muscle, and the human mind.

MAN.EXE, besides having a multitude of positive solutions for human reactions, also has a few drawbacks. This reaction is part of the MAN.EXE system as a form of a defensive reaction, but, like our distant relatives, Neanderthals, we should not view this as a defect or flaw, but as a means of growth. The moment we become aware of this tool, we can use it to our advantage, and it is no longer an unwanted reaction to life's difficulties but an opportunity for growth. We are not born perfect; tools are given to us, an opportunity to achieve that perfection, and it's up to us whether we will succeed. I am also sure that there are no people destined for success and others who accept everything good and bad that life offers them, thinking it's all a matter of a higher power or fate. The limits and power of one man reach infinity. Who can limit the power of the mind and put a period on the perception of reality? In the infinity of the limits of our mind, we can see when, for example, we see how some perceive reality. In some illnesses such as schizophrenia or under the influence of opiates, the human mind can open up to new areas of reality, where other laws of physics prevail. When we dream, our reality is altered. We truly believe that our dream is true, that we are flying, fighting monsters, facing fears and threats, dying. Dreams are doors to an altered reality achieved naturally. So why not use the above-mentioned methods to change our reality, to create a more perfect being without non-existent inhibitions set by bodily limitations that do not exist. I won't mention the cliché here that each of us can achieve everything we want in life, and I won't delve into the delusions that are very popular today, where we have situations where morbidly obese people are called beautiful and healthy. No, this is about something else; there are means and tools for achieving greatness, but not an easy path to it.

"Power"

When I talk about this topic, I prefer to quote J.R.R. Martin, and his character Lord Varys in my favorite series Game of Thrones which says:

"Power resides where men believe it resides. It's a trick, a shadow on the wall, and a very small man can cast a very large shadow."

You can have physical limitations; you can be nobody and nothing, but at the same time, you can convince everyone that you have all the power in the world. That power doesn't come from a physical appearance but from the mind. Your mind, your perception of yourself, your behavior, your attitude, speech, tone of voice, gaze, walk, manners... Power, like money, cannot be created or taken, at least not legally. Power is something given to you voluntarily; power is the reaction of others to your presence. Know that when you demand power and respect, you won't have it. A lion doesn't have to convince other animals that it's dangerous. Other animals give him the right to be dangerous and powerful. Convince others that you are powerful, but do it with your presence and actions, not words. Others give you power voluntarily, and only then is it real. What is the definition of a powerful man? Each of us has a different definition based on the experience they have lived through. But if we were to imagine a powerful man, we would probably attribute some of these characteristics to him:

- Strong

- Wealthy

- Dresses well

- Doesn't talk much

- Confident

- Optimistic

- Has a beautiful and successful woman by his side

- Rational and clear

- Well accepted in society wherever he goes

- Radiates success

"Success and Wealth Accumulation through Business"

The question of the characteristics of a successful person is sometimes similar to asking what came first, the egg or the chicken. Do these characteristics stem from the fact that someone is successful, or is someone successful because they possess these characteristics? Success is exclusively a personal characteristic, a personal perception of oneself. A successful person doesn't pay much attention to whether someone else holds a perception of their success; simply put, it doesn't matter in their life. Sometimes the wealthiest people just dress casually, making it almost impossible to recognize them on the street. What we associate with success are the prejudices we attach to an imaginary person, a walking god of success. However, in all of this, there is one big "But" that can be used to manipulate others in our favor. As I mentioned, Power as a synonym for success is something that is given to us voluntarily. It's easy for a successful person to base their position of success not on the majority's opinion, but until they become successful, they must build themselves and their personality so that, in the end, their character and demeanor, whether they like it or not, take on the outlines of the successful person they dream of becoming one day. Of course, we're not talking about people whose success is based on their parents' wealth or sudden millionaires who didn't have time to develop the character of a true "hustler." I'm talking about millionaires from scratch, those who grew into millionaires by developing a business from nothing. Even born millionaires are generally not the brats from Hollywood movies as we often mistakenly imagine them. The vast majority become very successful people, good businessmen, family people. The generational experience of their parents is passed on to them, and at the same time, they have more time to deal with things like investments, fewer dangers of making mistakes, and more opportunities to learn to handle money. The 20 years that some of us will spend becoming rich struggle with the lowest but also the most numerous competition; they will develop their successful businesses. Many say that earning the first million is the hardest, and that's true. Imagine starting from scratch, building wealth from a few hundred thousand dollars. Anyone can do that, and many do. The problem is investing a few hundred thousand dollars because such investments don't go into risky businesses, dreams, and ideas but into well-thought-out combinations. The chicken-and-egg problem arises, and the question is whether you are rich because you know how to earn, or you know how to earn because you are rich. A business of a few hundred thousand dollars, and more, a few million, is not done with your own money.

What is always a mystery is where the line between wealth and poverty is, when do we become rich, even when we don't have a lot of money in the bank? What does this actually mean? Well, quite simply, a rich person will quickly become rich again, and a poor person will easily become poor even if they win a million in the lottery. Wealth is a skill that is built or learned. In general, it is easier for someone who has grown up in wealth because they have been consciously and unconsciously trained to be rich their whole lives. As I said, when you have a few hundred thousand dollars surplus or even a few million (surplus meaning you don't owe money but literally have a few hundred

145

thousand dollars to spare for investment), you can't do something crucial with that money, nor should you use this money for a business. The prerequisite is that you know how to earn it, and investing in a business from scratch is not a solution but investing in a well-established business. For such combinations, bank guarantees and loans are used. Banks have all the mechanisms to assess the success of business and investments. It's up to you to seize the right opportunities. It is much different, therefore, to work from scratch; usually, you start with your own money. You start with your idea, your work because it is the "cheapest," and you have as competition everyone who has a few thousand dollars to spare. This is also the biggest curse, but also the greatest opportunity to build the character of a businessman.

Rich people don't work for money. Rich people work with money. A good businessman doesn't worry if he will go to work tomorrow and if everything will fall apart because he can't spend 10 hours of his life every day for the business to grow. A good businessman will not get into a situation where his business is falling apart because his investment portfolios in various businesses either do not allow it or allow it, but the anticipated benefit is greater to even risk it this way. From my experience, there are 3 types of business people:

1. The lowest and most numerous layer of small dreamers who are willing to invest a few

hundred or thousand euros in a business, work day and night to make that business succeed.

2. The middle class of entrepreneurs and businesspeople, who are capable of investing a little more, with stable incomes, investments in real estate, and safer business ventures.

3. Businessmen - investors who exclusively work with money.

The lowest layer of businessmen is at the same time the most motivated but also the most stressed layer. They don't know much about business, but they want to try it, invest in something, work day and night, create millions from scratch, although very few actually do it, or they get attached to the product, spending decades struggling and creating this imaginary million. The lowest layer of businessmen has two important characteristics that do not allow them to move up from this level. The first is the lack of collateral. These businessmen usually do not own real estate. They start from scratch. Their credit rating is very poor, and even if they were to get a loan, the cost of it could not justify the investment because they invest "on a small scale." The acquired assets in the rest of their lives should not be risked because for decades, they have struggled to become successful, and the goal slowly does not justify the means. Even when they acquire some assets, they cannot break the cursed circle because the second characteristic prevents them - the mindset. The mindset of such businessmen is a limiting factor in their growth. They start from the position that every business must start from scratch to succeed. That we must have an original idea that no one else has to succeed, that we must give ourselves, our time, our whole being for the business to succeed, that there is no other way except hard work. These businessmen, even when they take a step forward, acquire assets - collateral, remain at the same level because they invest in similar businesses. They fall into traps because very often they do not value their work highly, even though they work 12 hours a day, and it is not possible to clone themselves. Then the first established business, now already somewhat successful business suffers because the second one quickly becomes unsuccessful, dragging the first one down because it suffers from the lack of exclusive control by the businessman.

The second type of businessman is that group of businessmen who have stable cash flows from businesses they have already established, have collateral but change their mindset unlike the first group, and slowly begin to resemble the third group of businessmen. They invest less in time-consuming businesses and more in developed businesses, proven investments, use banks and loans more, work with real estate. I often read advice from the rich that is based on motivation - work hard, have passion, motivation, if you don't work 12 hours, someone else will, you can, no one else... I'll tell you something a little different. Have you ever wondered why those wealthy people sit on social networks and motivate you, who are nobody and nothing to them? Have you wondered what their interest is in all of this? Are they helping? Okay, you want to help, set aside 10 million dollars, help 1000 small micro-businesses. 1000 families might succeed in achieving steady incomes. I am allergic to millionaires who sell their story by quoting that well-known saying to all of us, "Give a man a fish, and you'll feed him for a day; teach him to fish, and you'll feed him for a lifetime." How will a person learn to fish when the ship's captain persistently gives him only tasks like setting up the hook or cleaning the deck? The essence is that this first group of people is very necessary, both for the second and especially the third, the richest, to survive. We must look at society as a pyramid. At the bottom is pure consumerism, the poorest, living from day to day. Someone said very smartly that slave in ancient Rome worked and at the end of the day had food and shelter for himself and his family. Today, this poorest group works every day so that they cannot eat well or earn enough money to provide a home for themselves and their children. So, according to every possible description, these are modern slaves. Above them are micro-businessmen, who have dreams but not collateral and the mindset needed to change their micro-business status. They produce, can gain something from property in their lifetime, but not a lot. Above this group is the group of small businessmen I just spoke about, and at the top are big businessmen, the least numerous as a kind of small pyramid narrowing into infinity. Each top of the pyramid must have the best, strongest, and widest base. Without the middle, it can survive, but not without the base.

So, motivational speakers, online billionaires, and the world's most successful people should be your motivation, but only until you acquire collateral and mindset. From that moment on, forget about role models. Let your only motivation be money. From that moment on, it is possible to buy another property, and very soon a third, fourth, etc. When you have stable incomes from your business and stable incomes from real estate, you can think about big investments, which is a step further. Don't look at businesses from scratch anymore. You are no longer an entrepreneur; you are now a trader, but not with stocks but with businesses. Look for businesses that are secured by loans; if you have to invest your money, invest it in such businesses. Banks do not invest money in businesses that have no future, keep that in mind. You must recognize the risk of the business. Even if you don't go into extensive market research and the business itself that is offered, observe the investment realization and the estimated return time. Maybe it's possible to return the money in 3 years but ask yourself why someone is selling a business for such a low amount. If we take that a good investment in real estate returns in 10-15 years, aim for businesses that return in 5-8 years as the safest. When you have assessed the return on investment as realistic, then start with the business analysis. Don't invest in businesses that don't offer a salary to the owner but require only work. The company's value can be anything; there are companies worth millions with just one employee, but generally, there are some indicators that favor taking over a business. I'll mention just a few of them.

Real Estate

When a company owns real estate, that is a good indicator that some earnings and profit come from its operations. Still, real estate, in my calculation, is calculated with a coefficient of times 2. Yes, real estate is an asset, but real estate also means collateral. If the real estate is not used for current operations, it can be used to obtain new real estate, meaning that in the end, it represents a business within a business in my ultimate calculation. A good businessman does not allow his money not to be produced, so owning real estate within the company means that the real estate can be leased and based on it, a loan can be raised to buy another property and lease it. Real estate is always an indicator of the company's success, but also the last chance in case of the company's failure. When a company owns real estate, you can always secure your claims by extracting assets from the company. A good businessman always secures his claims first and then others, so he subordinates the company to his interests. A big mistake for beginners in business is that they often equate themselves with their company. The company is legally a separate legal entity from its owners. So, you should act accordingly. Your company is your most reliable client and should be treated that way. It is a client who will pay you first and put you in the first place ahead of employees, suppliers, and other individuals. Real estate can always be pulled out of the company with smart management and setting up the company correctly from the start. As such, it is one of the most important characteristics of the company's success.

The other assets

Another characteristic of a company's success is its other assets, such as machinery, tools, technology, and inventory. There are companies that lease everything from labor to technology. I'm not saying that such companies are not successful; some can earn millions. However, we are not talking about searching for uncut diamonds here but rather about businesses that can be traded. So, when a company has significant investments in technology that can be sold or, even better, separated into another company to reduce risks, that's a good sign. Of course, the prerequisite for all of this is anticipating business trends and effectively managing risks.

Inventory is also considered an asset, but caution is needed in this regard. There are significant fluctuations in product demand. Accumulating inventory often indicates poor management. When acquiring a company with inventory, consider the potential loss of these goods due to expiration, product recalls, redesign, etc.

The collapse of a company is not necessarily bad. It's bad if the failure is uncontrolled and unanticipated.

Employees

Having a larger number of employees at all stages of a company's operation is also a good indicator of a company's success. Employees are a kind of asset. They possess knowledge, and that knowledge comes at a cost. However, there is no company that doesn't have surplus employees. This is most evident in crisis situations when it's necessary to lay off, for example, 30% of employees for the company to survive. In most cases, the company does indeed survive by operating with 30% fewer employees. The question arises: were all those employees really necessary? Each employee can do at least 10% more, achievable through methods that don't create dissatisfaction. Thus, 10%-20% of employees are always potential surplus.

Regarding legal matters, a good lawyer in every company is unfortunately a waste of money and resources, also we need to question ourselves why a good lawyer is losing time in some company and not creating his own. Every lawyer can be replaced by an external law firm that handles all legal issues for more than 50% less money monthly. The same goes for internal accounting. All of these are potential savings and potential profit when considering the return on investment. From my point of view good lawyer will newer work for someone else rather then himself, and the most expensive lawyer is the bad lawyer.

Financial Statements and Due Diligence

Simultaneously, financial statements and the overall operation of the company should be observed, conducting both legal and comprehensive due diligence.

Mid-tier businessmen, unlike the lowest tier, change their mindset. A common problem in the lowest tier is attachment to the brand they've created. The mid-tier understands that a company can last only one day and can be passed on if profitable opportunities arise.

Return on Investment

When I spoke about the return on investment, I spoke generally about the potential indicator of success. If you need to hold an investment for eight years for it to pay off, then that investment is not good. The best earnings come from investing, renovating, and reselling. Stay in business for a year, two, three, and when you sell that business, you'll have a profit. Of course, set the price in line with the longer return on investment. The moment you invest in a business, the business is for sale. Whether it's a car you bought cheap, fixed, and put up for sale, real estate, or a company, the principle is the same.

The Wealthiest Businesspeople

The wealthiest group of businesspeople does not work on businesses with constant inflows. These are purely speculative businesses: trading companies, investing in funds and stocks, and making significant investments. They invest in people, businesses, and real estate. Their wealth is not in money; their companies may not have much profit, but they are highly valuable. Their money is not in a piggy bank or a bank; it's in foundations, in assets, in constant investing. Their investments are not in cash but in loans, the cheapest way for a large investor to obtain money.

As a modern man, this is your jungle. Your mindset is your hunting skill, and collateral is your spear. Unfortunately, many of us have to start from the bottom of the pyramid to reach the top, but each of us can reach that top. Very few separate us from that top. The average annual income to be in the top one percent of all people in the world is quite achievable. This only shows how strong the wealth pyramid's foundations are. Every man's instinct is to strive for the top, and our MAN.EXE can help us constantly by urging us to fight against beasts and humans. What's on us is to direct MAN.EXE. The moment you catch a rabbit, the first, the second, the third, provide just enough food so that your family won't go hungry; try with a wild boar, or a deer. Of course, there are those who will say, I'm good at hunting rabbits; my family is not hungry; I'll rest for a few days because I'm well-fed and comfortable. MAN.EXE is not something that leads us to the goal; MAN.EXE serves the journey, the struggle towards the goal, towards a new goal, and so on, until we are at the very top, defying the creator.

So, everyone has a goal. Every action is conditioned by having a goal. Similarly, the wealthiest have a goal: to ensure that their foundations are not undermined by the

155

awakening of the lower classes. That's why motivational videos mostly talk about the struggle, torture, fears, the need to persevere. Powerful people are not necessarily fighters. Powerful people are handlers. This means that a powerful person won't hit their head against a wall until the wall or head breaks but will find a way to bypass the wall. However, considering that most react to stereotypes of powerful people, it's easy for someone not so powerful, as Lord Varys says, to "cast a longer shadow" than they are. You don't have to be powerful to look like one, but understanding stereotypes of power and every other social dynamics hack should not be used aimlessly. Creating a caricature of a powerful person without a set goal will not benefit you. When it's useful is in specific situations like job interviews, business discussions, negotiations. A conversation about a job, a business discussion with a company, negotiations—these are situations where powerful stereotypes help. Don't pretend to be "powerful" for a day if you want to change your image; change it for real.

Some will say, how can I be rich every day when I haven't been rich for a single day? The answer is that the essence is not in wealth but in the feeling that you can. For example, how many times in life have unexpected significant costs arisen for which you don't have money? You simply feel that for some things in life, you don't have enough money, and your loved ones need or want them. For example, your car breaks down seriously just when you've covered all the "holes" in your financial construction, so you're at a positive zero. This positive zero often happens. You fall into such an inescapable situation that doesn't require much money, but you simply know that you don't have it now. The first feeling of a poor person is hopelessness, depression. Any somewhat proud man will react this way because "it's not about the money" but about honor, the erosion of the man in you, MAN.EXE in you is activated, entering a phase of despair but not having a spear to hunt rabbits, your hunt is more modern, there's nothing to catch. Now pause for a second. Turn off all these ugly, anxious feelings because how many times have you really been in such a situation, and you didn't die of hunger? Your body calls for action; your MAN.EXE seeks to get up, take a spear, and feed the family, but reality is different. You would like to solve all problems with one blow, immediately, now, to break the miserable feeling, but you can't because it's not realistic.

The solution is also unrealistic, but trust me, it works. Whenever I find myself in a situation with unexpected, impossible costs at this moment, I tell myself, "Oh, I'll earn it." I use that moment of despair; actually, it used to be despair, now it's the anticipation of new work, new earnings. This didn't develop immediately; the first few times, I convinced myself that everything would be fine and that I could earn it all, even though logically I couldn't. Then, when this premise hit accurately several times, my brain started reacting differently to "misfortunes" and "unexpected costs." Now I feel a slight adrenaline rush, practically happiness, excitement. Some will say that it still has nothing to do with reality because money can be earned or not; the old saying "stretch as far as you owe" isn't true. You can always earn more; you will always find a solution to the problem as you always do, but it's up to you whether your reality and the overall reality of everyone else observing you will be that you struggle with debts or that you enjoy life, gradually pushing the boundaries of living.

Millionaires don't keep millions in cash. They have more money in the bank, but their value is not in the money in the accounts. Very few have more than a million in accounts. Money is there to be a means of creating wealth, and wealth consists of real estate, companies, securities. A person like Elon Musk, who is now worth hundreds of billions, most likely doesn't have even 100 million in accounts. In fact, as stories circulate about him, he doesn't even have a million in accounts. Money in cash and accounts is kept for the functioning and operation of the business. Believe it or not, to live the life of a billionaire for one lifetime, you don't need billions. The most beautiful villas in the world can be bought for a few million, just like Bugatti and the most expensive supercars. As for clothing, food, hotels, not to mention how much all that is „peanuts" compared to the total value. Do you want a yacht? Fine, for a few million, you can compete with the world's biggest businessmen. There are wealth limits in the sense that for about fifty million dollars, you can have everything money can buy in the world. Therefore, money becomes useless, and values are in other things.

So, let's go back to that feeling of hopelessness. Fool yourself that it doesn't exist; convince yourself that it's not a feeling of depression but a challenge. Very soon you'll start to love that feeling because it will push you further. Men are inherently programmed to fulfill needs, as we said, but then MAN.EXE becomes lazy. It satisfies itself with the feeling that everything is enough and doesn't take a step forward. My suggestion to you is to find a person or a way to provoke this feeling. You can do it yourself in ways we talked about earlier or find a person who pulls you out of your comfort zone. Whether it's your wife, best friend, or someone else, be with people who will pull you beyond your comfort because then you will grow. The worst thing is actually being the person who controls all finances and who is the one pushing because everyone is comfortable. While your wife and children are satisfied, your MAN.EXE doesn't enter a state of necessity and struggle. The absence of need is more fatal to a man's growth than the presence of unattainable needs. A great need will make you at least get closer to that goal; the absence of need will make you stagnate, but in the long run, you will lose because you won't grow enough to be competitive.

You know that feeling that you can retreat to the woods, live off your two hands, in seclusion without contact with other human beings. Man in his basic form, without needs, is exactly like this. The needs of our loved ones, not ours, have turned self-sufficient hermits into soldiers, statesmen, businessmen. The needs of our wives, children, parents, and then status and respect have created civilization from aimless hermits. I know that all men reading this will understand, especially those with families, our needs are insignificant. Because of our personal needs, we probably wouldn't move out of the house; it's because of the needs of our wives, children, parents, and then family, which is an additional motivation permeating every moment of our existence.

"Mental Health of Men and Challenges of the Modern Era"

Depression, or what we commonly refer to as depression in today's world, I feel the need not to label as a mental illness. I've had the opportunity to encounter individuals in life who suffer from anxiety, often accompanied by depression as a constant companion. Additionally, in my work, I've faced various types of people, including those with mental disorders, schizophrenics, and individuals with various psychoses. The boundary between mental illness and disorders has always been clear to me, at least my boundary, as I don't delve into neuropsychiatry. I don't know enough to speak about it, so I don't want to misinterpret the entire field.

The depression I'm referring to, which we all experience to some extent, especially men, is a disorder that arises from placing a man as a human being in a system that naturally contradicts his basic human functions. The depressed man is essentially the mouse from Universe 25, an individual who doesn't fulfill his life function even though his basic life program tells him he must. The depressed man of the 21st century is the overweight IT professional who works only at night for an American company, has no girlfriend, drinks Coca-Cola, eats via delivery, and mostly sleeps during the day to work at night. Variations on this theme are numerous, but fundamentally, it is a person who is not physically capable of defending himself and his family. It is someone who is an undesirable sexual partner, who doesn't fulfill the biological purpose of reproduction, doesn't provide for the family, has no contact with people and nature. A "universe 25" shell vulnerable to manipulation, indoctrination, capable of proving its "power" in ways that defy nature (mass shootings, for example). He is, in fact, a weak person, unwilling to change anything even though every cell in his body calls for change and a return to a natural state.

Firstly, if we are not talking about depression as an illness but as the social depression of the 21st century man, the solution is to return to nature. Start with the gym, build your body for at least 6 months until we get used to the feeling of physical existence as men and develop the necessary physical condition to theoretically defend ourselves and our loved ones. In addition, it is necessary to change other elements of our lives that make us socially depressed to return to the natural state of things.

On the other hand, depression and any mental illness must be addressed with therapy. From experience with people who have a wide range of diagnoses, I know that the only way to "fix" a mentally ill person to the extent that they become a member of society is therapy, whether psychological or pharmacological – that's the job of a psychiatrist.

What is necessary is to be aware of our mental state. Understand what makes us depressed. This is especially important because men are more likely to commit suicide. Men silently suffer within themselves to avoid being stigmatized by society. If it's about social depression, change your lifestyle. If it's an illness, seek treatment. It is crucial in today's time to be aware of our health. Unnatural occurrences, cheap substitutes for basic life needs, force our minds to adapt. Many fail, and even those who succeed eventually realize that this state is unnatural, producing a negative counter-effect after some time. There is often a saying that only those who have never been to a psychiatrist have no mental illnesses. Just like our body, health, and diet, our mind and mental health must be perfect if we strive for excellence.

The biggest problem when it comes to the mental health of men is their innate inability to express feelings. When I talked about the way of showing emotions and differences between men and women, I only touched on the emotional state of men. Men and women feel the same emotions, as the same type of living beings. I refuse to believe that there is any difference in the amount of love a man can feel compared to a woman. So why is there often a belief that men are colder and more reserved, and that women love more passionately? If I had to create an equation for giving love, it would be like this: given love = feelings - inhibitions. Inhibitions, by definition, involve the retention of some organic action, function, by will or involuntary physiological action.

"MAN.EXE" is precisely responsible for the existence of far more inhibitions in men than in women. Although men are often accused of not providing enough love to women, that very behavior is what attracts those women. Of course, it's a paradoxical stance, but if we historically establish the reasons for the existence of inhibitions and why they are attractive to the female gender, the existence becomes quite understandable.

If we take an example of a proto man, such as a Roman emperor or any ruthless ruler, we can analyze why certain behaviors that are equivalent to emotional inhibitions today are actually masculine and part of the "MAN.EXE" basic male program.

Our imaginary emperor doesn't talk much. When he says something, his opinion is a divine message.

"He listens, doesn't make decisions hastily" - our emperor knows he is a human being. He knows he can make mistakes and understands that the only way to make the right decision starts with the premise that he possesses all the information. He must not make mistakes. The moment he makes a wrong decision, he loses authority over his subjects, and that's why he must be ruthless even when making mistakes because dead men tell no tales.

"He doesn't make an effort to show love in the circle of others" - our emperor must be ruthless. Our emperor must not show happiness; happiness is a weakness. A weakness because it shows that these people matter to him, shows that losing them could harm him, influence his decision-making. Our emperor is still a human, a man who cares for his loved ones and is aware of the danger that attachment to them exposes them to. He strives to be strict towards his children but at the same time to be their idol. He doesn't hug, kiss, and caress his wife in the presence of others." - the absence of inhibitions calls into question the judgment of our emperor. Will he be an ideal ruler, will he be able to overlook the childish demands of his closest ones to make a fair decision? Will he be able to, in 15 years, lead an army and quell a rebellion initiated by his son, watching him die to protect the empire above all? Will he be able to send him on a campaign and thereby share the fate of his subjects - convince them that he didn't send them to die in vain? As a father and husband, he knows that his loved ones are his greatest weakness and the danger they face is significant. He strives to be strict towards his sons, demanding that he be more of an idol than a father because that's how he creates future emperors, not spoiled princes.

"He reduces emotions mainly to being present at meals, sexual relations, and sleeping in the same bed. He doesn't talk about raising children, household needs, arguments, and his wife's personal problems. He seeks respect" - our emperor is under tremendous pressure. He cares about the lives of all subjects; every word he utters is evaluated, every move and stance. Our emperor seeks peace. Peace is all he needs because it recharges his batteries, it's his vent. At the dining table, he sees the results of his successful reign - happy, strong, smart children. A beautiful, healthy, and smiling wife. He feels that his role is to keep them that way, to be crucial to their well-being. This is his relief valve; this fulfills him. He doesn't bother with minor things because his decisions have enormous consequences.

Many will wonder what a king or emperor has to do with modern men. Others will say that this his wife uses him and that she is with him because he is a emperor and has money, not because of love. The truth is somewhere in between. Only those who superficially look at the behavior of our emperor will judge him. Our emperor is, above all, a man who functions at the most basic level and then a ruler who is aware of the consequences of his actions. But, being a emperor and an ordinary man of the 21st century are different things, aren't they? Well, not really. You've surely heard the expression "everyone thinks their own burden is the heaviest," and it's like that. Poor and millionaire have the same stress level regarding their problems. Yes, it's easier for a millionaire because he has money... No! Problems affect all of us equally; the stress hormone is secreted in any case, be it financial, health, or other problems. Yes, objectively, some problems are more significant than others, but that doesn't mean subjectively they don't hurt equally. So, our modern man, like every man from the beginning of the world, is in the middle of a struggle every day. A struggle for partners, for dominance, for survival. This struggle affects him just as much as those who are much more successful than him. A king or a peasant essentially have the same problems; objectively, some of the problems are more significant. Subjectively, a king and a peasant will react the same.

As a man strives for success, for a name, for wealth, he doesn't do it for himself. He does it for his family and ultimately for the legacy he will leave for future generations. Even when a man strives for success, he does it for his family and ultimately for the legacy he will leave for future generations. This might not always seem like that, especially to the female gender, who might not fully understand these male impulses. Someone might say he bought a Lamborghini for his children, sure... NO, he bought a Lambo for his status, bought a Lambo because he wants to attract potential partners, bought a Lambo because it opens up connections with people who also have a Lambo, and bought a Lambo because for the next 100 years people will talk about how A.A. succeeded in life to the extent that he drove that Lambo while creating a lasting advertisement for his children for decades to come. Although it might not seem that way because to the casual eye this looks like a selfish move, but looking at it from a different perspective, a Lambo is an investment and a good one, maybe a brilliant one! Status is an incredibly important thing for men. A man is a conqueror; he wants to be talked about, he wants others to admire him, for women to look at him with desire. This innate desire for perfection, even when it's sometimes objectively impossible, is what attracts.

Our queen may not understand every time the motives and reasons why our king behaves this way, but surely this behavior will unconsciously attract her, create a sense of security and pride towards him. The emperor and empress will love each other until the end of their lives, even though they live unimaginably in today's time.

As the modern era is an era of conversation, an era of open expression of feelings, a man in his original form is forced to lose an important part of his attitude, a part that was instinctively very attractive to women. Striving to understand each other and to get closer, the sexes have become even more separated. It's not by chance that in our language, male and female are called the male and female genders, not referring to sexual characteristics. Male and female are like the poles of a magnet; a magnet is not a magnet if it doesn't have both poles. Maybe I'm exaggerating all of this a bit, but male and female, to be attractive to each other, must preserve a level of mystique that is incredibly difficult to maintain in today's age. Too much talk about feelings makes a man seem feminized, too much talk about fears makes a man weak, too much talk about finances makes a man financially unstable, too much talk about mental state makes a man unstable.

At last, we come to the conclusion that the instinctive nature of a man to conceal his feelings, anxieties, and fears, on one hand, is necessary for him to be a man, but on the other hand, it increases the secretion of stress hormones, endangering a man's mental well-being. If a man neglects his instincts and basic principles of the MAN.EXE operating system, he enters another extreme, becoming undesirable for the female gender or the majority of women who do not neglect woMAN.EXE. He becomes weak, unstable, insecure, and again enters a vicious circle of stress, depression, and mental illnesses.

The nature of men is for them to conceal problems and deal with them with the words "be a man." We accumulate more things within ourselves and are capable of not talking about them, yet somehow manage to fight and find satisfaction in that struggle. On the other hand, women have to talk about their problems; they overcome them more easily if they share them. Their nature, being the weaker and gentler gender, is not endangered, in fact, a woman enhances her quality as a partner by sharing her feelings. It may sound strange, but seeking help and being the weaker gender is feminine and triggers the male "chivalry hormone", making it desirable. The problem arises when modern women of the 21st century, driven by the culture of equality, try to be "strong" to prove they can deal with the same problems as men. On the other hand, they expect men to open up emotionally and mentally. Thus, they adopt masculine characteristics themselves, while simultaneously striving for their partners to adopt some feminine characteristics. At that moment, an effect similar to trying to connect two same-pole magnets occurs; they naturally repel each other.

I must admit that I often do not understand women's aspirations for equality. This question ceased to be a question of financial equality and equal opportunities long ago. These two are undoubtedly essential in the modern age, equal opportunities for each of us, whether male or female, black or white, must be unquestionable. The problem arises with modern feminist movements that aim to equalize the male and female at the level of being, at the level of consciousness. Creating a universal gender, so they lose everything that attracted them to the opposite gender. This is fertile ground on which depression and mental illnesses thrive. This is true for both men and women.

A woman is a cure for every man. Women often do not understand this and seek confirmation of male love in words, actions, gifts, but the greatest confirmation of male love for a woman is what a man will do in moments of peace. If your man wants you by his side in the last moments of the day, if he hugs you tightly in bed, if he places his head on your chest, know that his love for you is unparalleled. The cure for male depression is a woman, and I state this responsibly. I also affirm that two minutes of peace with a woman you love, with your head on her knees or chest, are more effective than all calming medications combined. Similarly, the sense of security that a man creates for his woman will alleviate all anxieties and worries. Women have other methods, such as talking to friends, family; men don't, and any disclosure by a man will deepen his problem. This is also one of the main reasons why male depression is so prevalent and why men account for 80% of suicide victims.

The affirmation of a man's masculinity is reflected in his success. A man is a victim of his success. In nature, among animals, not all males are necessary; only a part is successful enough to reproduce and pass on their genetics to the next generations. Natural selection chooses the best male among lions, for example, so that the pride has a prosperous future. All male lions, after three years of life, are expelled from the pride and begin the struggle for life and the creation of their pride. The vast majority die of hunger in a short period. Only a few survive and become successful enough to one day overthrow the older pride leader and thus become the rulers. So, to survive and reproduce, a lion must be incredibly successful, fight, wait for his moment to become the pride leader. If a lioness fulfills her role in the pride by giving birth to offspring, she has fulfilled her purpose as a female being. For a man, his role can only be fulfilled if he is successful enough as a man. Unlike lions, it is much easier for human beings in terms of conditions and consequences, given that in most cases, human beings adhere to the principle of monogamy.

Besides being more prone to developing depression, the male gender is also more likely to sustain depression because very few men will talk about their problems and seek help. There is an incredible video circulating on the internet that strongly resonates with each of us. It is a survey with the question, "Be honest, who do you call when you are in the toughest moments, who is that one person you confide in?" Answers include: "No one, I am a man, no one cares," "not a soul, no one," "no one because I am completely alone," "I think I speak for many people when I say, no one," "no one, I am a man, no one cares about me," "what, do you call someone," "no one, I am a man." Is it necessary to change this? Is it necessary to influence men to open up, to unburden themselves of their problems? I will try to answer this, primarily addressing the female gender, despite avoiding sexist themes.

Step out onto the street, look at the building where you live; men built it. Look at the streets, bridges, planes flying in the sky, fields that are cultivated and tidy, countless cars flowing like rivers through the streets. Men created all this because their nature does not allow them to be dictated by the difficulty of the endeavor; they do it because "IT NEEDS TO BE DONE," not because it is easy or because they love it but because it is necessary. Necessary for their families to be safe, for their children to live in prosperity, and to create examples and goals for generations to come. These men, irreparable workers, slaves of their ambitions, created all this because they are men. Because their nature is like that. So, instead of trying to "heal" them by feminizing them to the extent that future generations will not want to be soldiers, firefighters, hunters, sailors, builders, it is enough to take their tired hands at the end of the day, their rare hair, and tired head from worries, put it on your knees, and grant them peace. You will have a wonderful marriage, with a man beside you who would give his life for you because it is his duty, and a mentally healthy person beside you!

Giving an answer to men on how to deal with these problems that affect all of us regardless of status is challenging but not impossible. There are no easy solutions, no magic wand to chase away problems, make others understand us, improve your relationships with your wife, family, and other people. There is only one way, believe in yourself, work on yourself, be the best possible man, and only then will you prove to yourself that you have done everything to achieve peace. Yes, conversation currently solves the problem, but in the long run and if used too often, it creates other problems. Giving up is not characteristic of us men; you must not give up on life, no matter how difficult it is, no matter how hopeless the situation may seem. The fact that we can breathe and look at the sky is reason enough to live. No problem is big enough, no condition is severe enough to take our own lives, but if you still feel that way, seek professional help. Rise and continue the fight until it begins to please you, until small victories become sweet, and the taste of blood is good. Your fight is you; never give up.

"Man and Money"

What does money mean to you? For our prototypical man, money has no value because it is a product of a more recent part of history, yet it is crucial for every man. Man is a natural provider; as we have seen, the basic instincts of a man are tied to providing for the family, yet men don't stop there. Is money an inseparable part of every man, no matter how strange it sounds? The first question we must ask ourselves is what money means to us personally. How do we perceive money, what feelings do we have towards it? It may sound a bit strange when we talk about feelings towards money, but I will explain quickly.

Mike lived in a wealthy family. From his early childhood, he had everything a child could wish for, and his sister Iris as well. Mike's parents were caring but did not make an effort to explain to their children where the money came from, how Mike and Iris had the most beautiful toys, went to the best schools, and ate healthy food. Living in disinterest regarding money and earnings, but socializing in completely different social circles, Iris and Mike developed two opposing attitudes towards money. Iris, socializing with friends whose parents were poor, developed a special sense of values from an early age. Every toy, every birthday, every gift Iris received in her youth, she appreciated, rejoiced in it, and developed gratitude because she had the opportunity to see the true value of gifts for those who do not receive them. On the other hand, Mike, socializing exclusively with rich children of the same social class as himself, did not develop this relationship with money. Every gift to him was mediocre because he could buy it himself; he was aware that money was abundant, and he could get everything he wanted. Consequently, he developed a feeling of indifference towards money.

David, Iris's friend, grew up in extreme poverty, watching his parents struggle to earn some money, a concept he did not understand well. Son of a farmer, grandson and great-grandson of farmers. He learned to appreciate the fruits of his hands and his land. Always looking at the sky even when, after 25 years, he moved to a big city and worked an office job. One day, just a week after walking with his father through endless fields of agricultural products, dreaming of a new combine, of the life that would follow this year's harvest, which was one in 10 years, as his father said, while the warm summer breeze swayed the still-green wheat... He remembers this day even today. And then the next one, standing in the hallway, with open exit doors overlooking the swaying wheat in the field, watching his parents shed tears, semi-crouched, embraced because that is all that remained for them, while the hail mowed down ripe peppers, juicy summer watermelons, and the wheat that had swayed so beautifully in the wind now painted streaks with grains of immature wheat.

"Now the bank will take our farm because we don't have the money to repay the loans," his father cried out. Trying to comfort him, he took out his pocket money, but it produced even greater sadness in his parents. From that day on, David viewed money as something bad. With a heavy heart, even though after a few years he almost forgot about that day. Money is bad; only evil bankers, politicians, and speculators have it. David was hardworking, and that was the greatest wealth he took from his family, but his attitude towards money never helped him earn more than he needed to survive in his life. Inside him, he unconsciously struggled with the feeling that if he became rich, he would be like those evil bankers who took the farm from his parents, that abundance of money is wrong and evil. He struggled with the world but also with himself throughout his life.

On the other hand, Mike grew up to be a successful businessman. The family wealth was too great for his indifference towards money to have an impact. In 2008, the global economic crisis began. The family company built by generations of their parents was facing bankruptcy. He had no understanding of the changes, believed that everything would fix itself. He did not accept the fact that wealth was disappearing rapidly, continued to live a lavish lifestyle as he was used to, until the moment of bankruptcy finally came. At that moment, he felt resentment; he did not understand how this could happen, how to move on, why banks did not want to give him loans. He was angry with them, angry at the whole world, feeling that it owed him, that it was not his fault that the global crisis occurred. He hated the government, he hated everyone who did not give him what was "his."

Unlike her brother, Iris, in her childhood, although living in absolute wealth, developed a sense of value. She did not see gifts through the lens of money; she did not see her clothes in terms of money but as a collection of values she felt from the person giving her the gift and herself. Yes, a cap embroidered with the initials I.N. did not have much value for her, and she could buy hundreds of the same, even hire a seamstress to embroider initials on all her caps. Still, for David and his mother, that gift meant wealth. Iris felt this throughout her life and learned how much gifts are worth to the one giving them. Not just gifts, anything, even that product imported from China for a few dollars, she knew how to assess that the value written on a piece of paper next to it as its price was not the value of the product itself. It included the work of probably underage Chinese workers with very low wages, the cost of its transportation to the USA, marketing, logistics, rent of premises, the cost of labor, but also the profit of the owner. Iris developed into a good businesswoman, knowing how to adapt herself and her business to the changing market conditions even during a crisis. Iris looked at money as energy. As a kind of nerd and physics enthusiast, she always compared money to energy. She said that money cannot be spent or disappear, but like energy, it can only be transferred from one body to another or transformed from one form to another.

I often have the opportunity to say, "Tell me what you think about money, and I will tell you what kind of person you are." In this example, we saw how three different personality types, in two different life situations, can produce three different outcomes. Just because someone is born rich does not mean they know how to handle money, nor does someone born a poor farmer mean they will continue the tradition of their ancestors. However, if we have a mindset like David, this unfortunate farmer's child, we will struggle and find it difficult to earn money while battling our own demons throughout our lives. I have spoken many times about money as a measure of value, a measure of success, but fundamentally, I have not spoken about the relationship with money. That relationship will be the determinant of our success but also something we can change if we want to be successful men.

How often have you had the opportunity to talk to famous deniers of everything, who often blame others for their financial situation, blaming the government. These people blame everyone else, the whole system is to blame, and then they often start with the story, "why do they need so much money, only money matters," etc. This group of people is like David; they actually hate money. They know they need it, but essentially, they hate it. They think money is something that corrupts, a foreign entity they don't need because they have ego and pride, and they can't be sold for a handful of coins, as if someone is trying to buy them. If these people happened to acquire millions, they would soon spend it. Money doesn't change anything in their lives; they will live the same, whether they have it or not.

Understanding what kind of person someone is can be very easy based on how they react to gifts, especially gifts that have a deeper meaning. Will they accept that cap with initials with joy, understanding that someone had to sew it and spend their precious time, and ultimately thinking about that person, planning what to buy, and eagerly wanting to delight them with a gift? Or will they look at the gift through its financial value (like Mike), or consider the gift a burden, something bad because it creates the "obligation to reciprocate" (like David).

Money and man are inseparable. Money is to the modern man what tools, a comfortable cave, soft animal skins on which his family slept, prey, and food reserves were to Homo sapiens. Money is a measure of success, and today, when a man's success in our constant struggle with other men is no longer measured by broken skulls, shields, and broken swords, money is the best possible scale to measure success. Without success, goals, and victory over other men, a man cannot be considered a man. His pride and qualities are reflected, in part, through the state of his account and overall financial value. "MAN.EXE" directly links money as a measure of success with the psychological state of every man. Women, and even other men, can separate our qualities as successful, good people from the amount of money we have, but subconsciously, each of us will measure our quality through money. If our perception of our own value is much higher than what we are worth now, as well as any disagreement between the current and ideal state of things will create a sense of discomfort, ultimately leading to depression.

So, money is one of the measures of our own quality. We should look at money like muscles, social circles, lifestyle. Money and wealth are built; it's not easy to earn and succeed, but our basic male program tells us that it's necessary, that we must compete and be the best. It does not accept that there are billions of people in worse financial situations, all because there is 1% in the world who are better off than us. This is both beautiful and damned in our basic program, as it drives the poor son of a field worker to become the new millionaire, it's what continues to drive billionaires to be the best, and the richest man in the world to leave a legacy for all future generations.

What should the attitude toward money be? Each of us looks at money, its value, and the way it is spent differently. As I mentioned, some see money as something bad, associating the possession of money with a bunch of bad people, bankers, criminals because, besides crime, it's not possible to "honestly" earn. Others like to behave like hoarders. They earn a lot but don't spend, don't invest, collect "dollar on dollar," expecting to be millionaires one day, which they eventually become, but they reach a point where it is irrelevant to the quality of their life. Besides, with their misunderstandings, they incorrectly train generations inheriting money, so they don't know what to do with it. Some start with senseless spending of the inheritance because you only live once, and others go to the other extreme, living the same way as before. Poverty is the result of a poor mentality, not a lack of money. The lack of money is only a consequence of a poor mentality and nothing more.

Now we come to the main question: how should we look at money? Personally, I prefer to look at money as a kind of energy. Money comes and goes, flows like a river, and moves towards other rivers. Don't get attached to the banknote, to the cash register, to money for rainy days. Your goal is for your inflow to be greater than the outflow; that is the simplest description, but not sufficient for a fundamental understanding of money. Your money is the energy that moves. With your money, you move other people, other businesses; it's just a moment at your place and then serves others. Although it sounds a bit strange, from the current point of view, I believe that the goal is not to have money reserves but to have no money at all after distributing it to other machines, businesses, and people. The most effective way to distribute money is to distribute it all, not for consumption but for investment. The cost of money that stays in one place without further use is much higher than investing or distributing it. For this reason, billionaires don't have a lot of cash in some cases; their wealth is in other values, companies, real estate. In fact, they often don't even have anything in their name. They register companies in trusts, establish associations, and foundations. All these are methods to get rid of money because they know that standing money is expensive. Firstly, it loses value because it stands, as inflation "eats" it more every day, and secondly, the fact that you as an individual have come to physical money already speaks to the price you've paid for holding it in your hands. Salary is heavily taxed; company profits are also taxed. For every transaction you make, you pay VAT and other taxes. During all this time, the same money loses value due to inflation, and eventually, you don't even use it in physical form, but as the pinnacle of stupidity, we use a card that reduces the energy and value of money for us because the bank takes a commission for that transaction. However, this also affects the business into which we bring energy with our money because their inflows are reduced.

If we put on paper how much we lose every time we choose money over some other value, it would roughly be like this: if our gross salary is 1000 euros, net is 550 euros, that's what we get in hand when taxes and insurance, and pension contribution, are paid. Someone will say, yes, that's correct, but at least I'll have a pension when I get old. But we will get to that; with these 550 euros, you pay property tax because it's also part of life, pay bills to the state, pay for food and other necessities; VAT is calculated on everything, which is in most cases 20%. So, you end up with 450 euros reduced for taxes and fees that are not part of consumption but simply fees that the state takes; you're left with 350 euros. So, the initial energy of money of 1000 euros has flowed into other companies with the energy of only 350 euros. Of course, this calculation is quite simple and unrealistic, a bit exaggerated for easier understanding, but fundamentally, the value of this 1000 euros you receive at the end is worth a little more than 300 euros. What are the alternatives to a salary? Well, essentially, you have to have some salary; that's why it's always the hardest for the poorest people who are most heavily taxed. Perhaps not the highest, but the hardest because the blow is greatest on the salary, and that's all these people have. So, you can't avoid having some salary because you have some basic living costs to cover. However, in the variant that you are your employer, that is, you own a company, you can avoid paying a salary, use the company's money for a good part of basic needs, and thus reduce the need for cash because the company can always offset costs with taxes, so in the end, the company is on the so-called "positive zero," enabling further borrowing but preventing the state from collecting taxes. Holding property as company property is perhaps the best thing you can do to protect your personal property and reduce costs. A house that is part of your company's property is secured from personal bankruptcy, also exempt from division in case of divorce, all maintenance costs can be borne by the company, so that cost also goes to the company's expenses, and therefore, it reduces potential taxes. In this way, the energy of money is retained at 80%-90%, and even VAT can be offset with invoiced VAT. All this also benefits other companies that also retain the energy of the received money in full, so they can distribute it further. Offsetting receivables is also a great way to maintain the value and energy of money. Look at the value of the company as the salary you receive but for which you don't pay any taxes. Every cent of increase in the value of your company is your money. If you work for someone else, choose to receive your salary in stocks. It's foolish to pull out a million-euro salary and pay 50% tax for it; it's also foolish to pull out a profit at the end of the year, even though some countries tax corporate profits very little; it's still about taxed money, it's still about money that loses value every day and that must be spent and taxed. Don't shy away from loans; it's the cheapest money there is, but of course, not cash loans for consumption but investment loans. Look at the bank as a free assessor of your company's success. The bank will not invest its money in something it thinks has little chance of success. You've already done a good part of the job if the bank, as a financial institution, approves your project; the rest is just up to you.

So, even though money as a means of payment is relatively recent, it is essentially a measure of a man's quality. I don't mean the spiritual side, character of the person, there are wonderful people who simply aren't rich, and that's okay. But the measure of quality in the sense of the quality of that person as a man, as a suitable person for reproduction, as someone capable of taking care of the family, to create and successfully raise offspring, and in some organic sense, to ensure that his family does not die of hunger, be killed by conquerors, to have a safe place to live. When women look at men with money, they subconsciously have these characteristics in mind. Yes, there are women whose only goal is money (although we can argue about this), but if we gave any woman the choice to start a family with someone who has a solid personality and lots of money, or someone who has a wonderful character but is without money, regardless of how much money she herself has and how successful she is, she would choose the first option because instinctively she believes that the first man is more capable of creating and sustaining a family with her.

We often say that a man's qualities are judged based on success, and women's are not. If a woman doesn't see in you the ability to create a quality future for her, no matter how attractive you are, you stand no chance of staying in that relationship. This might sound harsh, but a man must be slightly "better" than his woman. Every woman in the history of humanity has sought "quality" in a man, a better personality than hers, greater survival skills than hers, more money. A man can absolutely be satisfied and establish a family with a homeless person, a cleaner, a girl without education, without money, even with not particularly brilliant character. Why is that? Some will say it's about high or low standards; some will say men are sadists, aiming to oppress women and maintain their superiority complex by considering themselves more valuable than the woman "below" them. In reality, it's not like that. The essence is that in such situations, our basic instincts actually drive us.

MAN.EXE compels us to find a person who will take care of our children, not someone who will go to the moon and become a world-famous astronaut, or someone who will have to work 18 hours a day to succeed in their multimillion-dollar business. Our children need a safe home, food on the table, care, and nurturing, and that's what unconsciously drives us. Some men understand this and stick to the reality of these principles, so we call them chauvinists, while others are hypocritical and tend toward the other extreme.

To be clear, I don't believe a woman should stay at home, cook meals, and take over all the care for the children. My marriage is not like that; my wife is a successful businessperson, and sometimes, like any modern man, I take more care and raise my children, and that's okay. But that doesn't mean I'm unaware of what instinctively drives us men. Women, as naturally emotionally intelligent beings, beings we cannot match in verbal terms, often strongly defend the opposite view of their natural positioning with the family. But fundamentally, throughout their lives, they seek someone to whom they will be subordinate. I don't mean literally subordinate, but they can hardly stay in a relationship with someone who is worse than they are, and then they seek someone to take care of them, which is absolutely contrary to what they actually say defending their stance on independence.

Money is a measure of quality, energy, an indicator of a man's value. Money is the most banal indicator of success, not an indicator of personality quality, kindness, but certainly one of the criteria that make a man desirable. In addition, someone who has a healthy relationship with money can do many good things with it.

Money, besides being an individual measure of success, is a measure of society's success. Each of us is obliged to justify our existence on a personal level and be the best possible version of ourselves. Only such a man is good to himself, a steward to his family. His family, as the basic building unit of society, becomes a producer of value. A modern man must not be bound by the 20th-century views that hard work for an employer can lead to a decent life and a good pension in old age, which probably won't exist when you reach that age. The 21st century erases all outdated socialist ideas of society based on the recovery of society as a whole after world wars and ideological conflicts. The 21st century puts the individual, the entrepreneur, the small businessman in the spotlight.

Microbusinesses are the future. Every family member should strive for microbusinesses that grow into larger ones and ultimately create generational wealth. Instead of working for someone else, think about your skills, what you can produce, what services you can provide, and start your own business. With the growth of your personal wealth, the wealth of the family as a whole increases. Always keep in mind personal "GDP" and family "GDP"; the growth of these figures on an annual basis is a measure of your success, and at the same time, you as a man, as the head of the family, as the host, as an essential individual in society as a whole. The one who earns more can spend more and thus distribute prosperity to all other members of society.

Let's put aside politics and economics as a science. We must look at the growth of our wealth through a way of creating value with our hands from resources. We can do this by working for an employer and getting a salary, but then we must know that only a small part of the value of our work goes to us. In fact, the employer gets the largest part of our work, using that work to pay for marketing, management salaries, and ultimately profit.

When we cross this knowledge with the previous one about the energy of money, we get the following diagram:

TOTAL ENERGY WE CREATE

- Company Profit

- Marketing

- Resources for work

- Management salaries

= GROSS SALARY

- Taxes and contributions

= NET SALARY

- VAT
- Various taxes beyond real consumption

= FINAL CASH VALUE

Earlier, we learned that less than half of the energy of money remains from gross salary to get to the net salary, and by spending it, a good part goes not to consumption but to taxes. To get to the gross salary, in fact, the energy of our work is reduced to at least 1/3, and that's if we're lucky. The basic rule I adhere to in business, like many others, is that when hiring a new employee, the expected profit from that one employee is 2x his salary. So we hire an employee when his gross salary is equal to a 1/3 increase in income from that employee.

Working for someone else, in a large system, you are left with less than 10% of what you create with your hands and energy. Some will say that this is true, but if it were so easy to create a corporation that would provide us with a job, everyone would be entrepreneurs. There is history, decades if not centuries of market struggle, billions of investments, a lot of knowledge, etc. All this is true, but it is also true that each of the founders of these corporations is, above all, a human being, born as a blank slate - tabula rasa, that he had to start from somewhere, from zero, that he had to walk his path to become better, that he grew every year and eventually created an empire. Why shouldn't that be you? Who guarantees that you won't be a billionaire in 20 years from today? Why give up from the very beginning and settle for being a mediocrity?

It's time to see yourself as a company, your family as a company. Use your companies to turn consumption into profit. Every dollar of your company's consumption goes as pure consumption. This means that the company is taxed only on profit, i.e., what remains when all costs are subtracted from returns. Comparing it to a salary, it would be the same as getting a gross salary, then spending it all month, and at the end of the month, paying taxes on what's left. That's why the goal of every corporation is to be at a positive zero, which is an ideal situation because this way, the corporation does not pay tax on profit. Of course, this is a book like situation; most corporations show a profit for creditworthiness reasons, but this is something that needs to be delved into more deeply for the reasons behind such financial policies of companies. Looking at your income and business in this way, you are the one creating generational wealth. Yes, it will be hard; sometimes you won't succeed at the start, but I believe there is no way not to succeed if you truly work on it.

"The Art of Enrichment"

I come from a relatively small market, a tiny country in the Balkans, and even here, I realized that success is achievable if you work for it. You will always find clients, you will always find a buyer for your product, but you will make beginner mistakes—mistakes you must make to gain a true perspective on how markets and businesses function. At that moment, you can start any business and eventually succeed.

Imagine, for example, living in the U.S., one of the largest countries in the world and the largest market. Currently, there are about 33 million companies and around 330 million residents in the U.S. When your product can be delivered to the other side of the globe within a few days, there are no limits to product distribution within a country. So, if you can't find enough customers among 33 million companies or 330 million individuals, depending on what your product is intended for, it's entirely your fault and no one else's.

One common mistake many make from the very start is starting with a small profit margin. Starting with a small profit margin requires a lot of customers to generate profit. If you start with a large profit margin, you only need a few customers, and trust me, you will find them among these 330 million. One of the well-known Belgrade lawyers joked, "It's better to take 500 euros from one client than 500 euros from 5 clients." Although this is somewhat sarcastic and said in jest, it is absolutely true at the most basic level. You should set your criteria and profit margins very high. You might have five times fewer potential clients, but over time, you will reach the same level of work for much more money. The calculation is very clear, and I will try to explain it in my legal practice.

Assuming that my minimum fee is twice as high as the real one, on a monthly basis, I will have, for example, three times fewer clients. The loss in the first year is as follows:

Lawyer A - Without increasing the service price:

10 clients x N = 10N

On an annual basis: 120N

Lawyer B - With a two-fold increase in the price of the same services:

3 clients x 2N = 6N

On an annual basis: 72N

The maximum client load per lawyer is 50 clients per month. The annual increase in the number of clients due to referrals and marketing is 1.5 times without increasing service prices because the influx of clients is stable. A large number of clients also means less time for marketing. For the lawyer with an increased price, it is two times, considering that his focus was more on marketing.

2 years:

Lawyer A: 15 clients x N = 15N x 12 = 180N

Lawyer B: 6 clients x 2N = 12N x 12 = 144N

3 years:

Lawyer A: 22.5N x 12 = 270N

Lawyer B: 12 x 2N = 24N x 12 = 288N

So, in the third year, the lawyer with a higher profit margin and almost half the clients achieves a higher overall yield, all while working much less.

Furthermore, understanding human psychology when making decisions is crucial. I don't want to reduce the question of earnings to simple mathematics because, in reality, it is never as straightforward as I have stated. The earnings of my law firm are such that "there is everything", as I like to say related to my clients; there are the smallest ones to those from which you can buy a car or an apartment. However, generally speaking, it is always better to overestimate the value of your work. I will mention only some of the psychological reasons why a buyer prefers to pay more rather than less.

1. **More means better:**

    The basic belief of every buyer is that a higher price means better quality services or better quality goods. Sometimes, this is not the case, but there are a million ways for a product to increase its value with just small changes. Whether it's packaging, ribbons, messages, specific quality labels (handmade), even though handmade is no longer a quality measure because machines do a far better and more precise job. The same goes for services, the approach to the client, the appearance of the office, offering food and drinks, anticipating potential future problems/services. All of these are ways to sell your product at a higher price.

2. **Have an idea of your market potential and the value your product or service has for individual buyers:**

This is where the marketing devil I mentioned comes in. We all try, through our marketing actions, to reach as many people as possible. Besides that, we also change people's awareness to expand the market. The basic nature of humans will drive us to think in this way, but play it smart, narrow down your market. You don't have to conquer the whole world from the start; start with 3 clients, then 6, then 12. Also, let marketing sell your products. Very often, fellow businessmen, when starting marketing activities, try to attract clients on all fronts but not on any sufficiently. Whether it's social media, ads, television, cold mailing... Keep in mind that there is a rule of potential client reaction in marketing, so a potential buyer, in a sea of ads, must be under the influence of an ad at least 5-10 times. This means that in your case, a potential buyer must see your ad at least 10 times to create an impression of the product's value. So, think when you ,run one Facebook campaign or one cold email per month. Will the potential buyer get the impression of value? Of course not. At most, you can remind an old customer to buy the product once more. Remember, for someone to buy your product, there must be at least a small need for that product, then they must be under the influence of your marketing consciously or subconsciously at least 10 times to create an impression of the brand or product's value. After that, they must be targeted with an ad at least once more to trigger the buying impulse. The higher the value of the product, the more times you have to target the audience, but the audience itself is smaller. So don't expect to sell a yacht with 10 Facebook views; simply, to create an impression of the brand's quality, the yacht buyer must see your ads from multiple sources over a longer time, many times.

3. **"The first buying paradox":**

I personally named this the first buying paradox, and it relies on the previous point. The buyer will always, when presented with two identical products with a huge difference in price, choose the more expensive one. The reason for this is the fear of the cheaper one, that is, the fear of deception. This buying paradox leads to the...

4. **"The second buying paradox":**

This paradox is even stranger than the first but very common in practice. When a buyer buys a much more expensive product from a selection of two identical products, they will defend their decision to buy the expensive one even if they are fully aware that they have overpaid. They will show everyone that their purchase is logical, smart, and desirable, encourage others to buy the same product at a huge price, and ultimately, buy again in the same way as before.

Whenever you have a buyer who has already received an offer from another seller before you, you will most easily get that buyer not by lowering the price but by increasing the price at least 3 times from the first offer. The moment you offer the same service for 3 times more money, the buyer is in doubt about whether the previous offer was realistic, whether it hides hidden costs, and whether it is primarily of sufficient quality. The fear of deception is so great that, in case that price is impossible for the buyer, they would rather give up the purchase entirely than choose a cheaper product. This is a win-win situation for you on a global scale; you may not get the money, but you will also prevent a direct competitor from winning you in the market and life competition.

There are hundreds of ways to boost sales. It's a craft learned throughout life. I believe that in assessing the value of your service, you should start with how much your service is worth to the buyer. One of the big problems with a poor mindset is that we often think about how much something costs, not what you get for that money. This is the basic problem that a poor person brings into their business. You must always look at the value your service or product has for the buyer, not for you and not in relation to similar products. For example, it is entirely fair to sell a smoking addiction treatment for 2000 euros. Smokers spend 300 euros a month on cigarettes, 3600 euros a year, and the health problems smoking will create are priceless. If I give 2000 euros today and get rid of the cost of 3600 euros a year, that is a fair offer. The fact that stickers with nicotine are sold for 20 euros will actually force a serious buyer to buy your overly expensive product that you produce for 20 cents. If we follow the two mentioned paradoxes, that person will, precisely because they gave so much money to quit smoking, have a 10 times greater desire to quit smoking. When other potential buyers ask him if your product works, he will praise it out loud because subconsciously he does not want to appear deceived. Following these rules, we can easily apply them to any product and multiply the returns tenfold.

I already mentioned it, but I have to emphasize it again. There is a very important difference between the understanding of the cost of your work by a poor and a rich buyer. A poor buyer will look at your price as an expense; they will come to your office and ask how much it will cost them. On the other hand, a rich buyer will ask what they get for that price. The difference is crucial, and it requires a different approach to the client. With a poor buyer, you are aware that they will try to find a way to get as much service as possible for the least amount of money. On the other hand, with a rich one, the moment you attract them to buy, you can sell more services than they needed at the time of contact with you. For a company lawyer, there is always work, whether it's a lawsuit, due diligence, or just giving advice to optimize work, avoid future legal problems. That's why it's desirable to have the right approach to the client; offering a lower price to such a client can sometimes even be repulsive.

The skill of making money is equal to the skill of hunting or building a dry and safe shelter. Money is one of the measures of your success as a man, and it is entirely understandable that it is very important to men. Do not pay attention to objections and advice that you should "live," that money is not everything in the world, and the like. Of course, money is not everything in the world, but as long as there is thirst, as long as there is a struggle in you to create an empire, do not give yourself leeway, enjoy success, push forward. Money as the antithesis of enjoyment is simply a misconception. Do you think rich people don't enjoy? That they don't have everything they want, that money is a burden around their necks and that it restricts them from enjoying? On the other hand, can you enjoy life if you are poor, if you worry about surviving the month, paying rent? Can you enjoy if you are aware that you are not using all the God-given opportunities available to you? That money is some obstacle to happiness is a useful means for: 1. those who are poor to justify their incapabilities and 2. those who are rich to keep the poor from being enlightened and striving for wealth. Why would a millionaire care about what some poor worker thinks?

The answer to this question is historical. One of the greatest deceptions since the moment religion was invented. Starting from the promised kingdom of God, through 72 virgins, to today's money is evil. It all actually stems from a basic assumption and the principle of the operation of the MAN.EXE program, that is, "there can be only one."

The principle of "There can be only one" is based on the assumption of a man's life struggle for dominance over other men. This struggle, the final boss in the game of life that we can never defeat, is the basic program of a man, a constant struggle for survival and the struggle to be better than all others. You are born as a derivative of the victory of one sperm out of a million and one egg cell, you fight for life, for a breast, for your mother's attention. Some animals eject weak offspring from the nest; for example, a stork throws weak offspring from the nest, a pig eats weak and sick piglets, other animals abandon their offspring, and not so long ago in history, even humans did this, although it is now unthinkable. You successfully survive your youth and then comes adolescence. The struggle for dominance among peers, the struggle for reproduction, and then the struggle to create a name, an empire. The life of a man is a constant struggle, and it is innate in the genetic code.

For this reason, some smarter men thought of using manipulations such as religion to divert others from the struggle, to promise them in return the kingdom of God in abundance. To divert others from the struggle for reproduction by promising them 72 virgins after death. To divert others from money and entrepreneurship by convincing them that it's better when they are poor because they won't have that evil and heavy burden around their necks.

The truth is entirely different, it's time to understand it if you haven't already. Rich people also enjoy life, and perhaps even more than the poor. They have families; their children are provided for generations. They live longer lives because they have the means and the possibility of quality treatment. Moreover, they have no conscience pangs about their status, and the moment they want to do something for other people, they have the means to do it. It's nice to be rich, don't run away from it, grab everything that has been given to you. Otherwise, you will live a naturally bad life, not so much because of a lack of money, but because of all the missed opportunities to embrace being the man that God created you to be.

"Trauma as a Catalyst for Success"

What is it that turns two cells, an egg, and a sperm, into someone like Marcus Aurelius, Leonardo da Vinci, Nikola Tesla... When did Nikola Tesla become Nikola Tesla, when did Marcus Aurelius predestine himself to be an emperor, when did Hitler embark on an irreversible path in forming his personality?

Remember, we are winners from the very beginning because we originated as 1 in a million combinations of sperm and egg, the fastest sperm, the most resilient... No, this is not entirely accurate. Firstly, without wanting to spoil the motivational energy flowing from this romantic love story of a single egg cell and a swift sperm rushing towards each other, from a biological standpoint, this view is completely wrong.

The egg cell has mechanisms to fight against sperm; in fact, dozens and hundreds of sperm reach it first, attempting to penetrate the membrane, and die in the process. Finally, a lazy, sluggish sperm walks into an unprotected part of the cell membrane, amid millions of fallen warriors on its way, at the moment when the female reproductive system has employed all measures to combat unwanted foreign organisms. Some might say this is a miracle, that we are the product of one sperm and one egg cell among millions of possible combinations... That is true, but we must fundamentally reconsider the way we view statistics and probability.

Yes, the probability is one in about 5 million, but the probability of fertilization happening is 1/1. The probability of our tire bursting and hitting another vehicle on a busy road is very high if we focus on the moment the tire bursts. On the other hand, the probability of hitting exactly the BMW M5 driven by Nikola Jovic from Novi Sad, sent to Belgrade by the director late last night, just when his phone rings to inform him that his dog is sick, right next to the restaurant where he proposed to his wife on this day five years ago, is very low. In fact, the more context we add, the probability becomes smaller and smaller. Simply put, the collision had to happen, and whether it was Nikola's or someone else's vehicle is not that relevant to the event.

We humans attribute a mysterious character to such events, looking at them overly romantically. Similarly, we use this moment of the creation of a living being as a motivational example, but is it even relevant which sperm fertilized the egg out of millions of possibilities?

Actually, no. This is not the moment when the future human being predetermines to become a world-renowned scientist or a serial killer. No one is born bad; those with more children know that there is a pattern in the behavior of children. They are like little robots who mostly develop their specificities and characteristics at the same age—when they stop having colic, when their teeth come out, when they speak their first words, and when they give you their first smiles. Your children are a reflection of you, and for them, there is mostly no proactivity, only reactivity. They react to your emotions, your behavior, hugs, stress, attention. That is what shapes their character, their intelligence. Of course, I am not talking about exceptional situations bordering on biopsychological disorders; there are children who, at a very young age, know multiple languages, memorize beyond biological limits—savants. So, we are the ones shaping their characters. Every touch, every moment spent with them creates a small piece of their personality.

The problem in raising children is the fact that their development is formed in an environment that does not create enough significant challenges to shape successful individuals in the future. From the moment of birth, a child is accustomed to having everything their way, and that is perfectly fine because who will spoil children if not us, right? Unlike, for example, an antelope whose offspring must immediately stand on its feet and run, a human being cannot survive without their parents. They will receive milk at the right time, their diaper will be changed whenever needed, a comforting hand will always be there when they learn to walk. They will get regular meals when they start "independently" eating. Their "good behavior" will be conditioned with gifts and sweets; we will create exactly what we shouldn't create from a child if we want them to have a bright future.

Then they go to kindergarten, where they are again put into a training system to perform actions like all other children. Today we paint a tree, the color of the leaves is green, the color of the tree is brown. The rabbit is white, the sky is blue, the sun is yellow... Elementary school teaches them rhymes they will never use, and for that, they receive a reward, just like a candy at the age of two in the middle of a supermarket tantrum.

Parents are, of course, proud. Our child has all straight A's, our child is the best in the class, our child passed all exams at university with straight A's, our child started working in a big company earning a decent salary, will get a raise in five years, our child had a child, but they will have to put it in daycare as soon as possible because both of them work full time, there are more expenses, our grandchild has all straight A's... The enchanted cycle, as some call it, the rat race. Your child is now part of the system, one of those mice from Universe 25 condemned to mediocrity. Why? Because their whole life has been taught to be part of that system, just that candies and A's have been replaced by pieces of paper with imaginary value, actually worth less than candies, somewhere in the range of grades on an elementary school report. Such a life, like Universe 25, creates an unnatural state. We are not destined for mediocrity; we are human beings, the top of the food chain, the top of intellectual abilities, we change nature, create, and are complete masters of our own existence as well as the entire living world on Earth. All scientific achievements, civilization, and society we have created were not formed by going around in circles and living like those mice through a maze of rewards, that piece of cheese that connects the ends.

What created Nikola Tesla? No, it wasn't two cells that coincided under one in five million combinations to such an extent and in such a way that a scientist was born. Nikola Tesla was born as Nikola, Nidza, Nikolica, but his environment, the entire family and social situation, is to blame for him becoming a scientist one day. However, when one day we add up and subtract our entire lives, we mostly come to the answer that is that one moment, a moment in time, the culprit for our entire life. I firmly believe that that moment exists in all of us, that one "catalyst," trauma or a happy event that set our life in motion, that directed all the grandeur of the combination of our genetics towards the current outcome. Was it, for Tesla, the moment when he barely survived cholera as a child, which had a significant impact on him because he became a great germophobe or was it the moment he avoided forced mobilization in World War I by fleeing to the mountains from where he practically immediately went to study in Graz. It's difficult to tie fate to one event in life, but each of us knows which turning point made us who we are.

That one trauma, whether it's the death of parents when we realize that we have no one to turn to and provide a safe haven, whether it's the moment of surviving a serious illness when we realize that life is too important to waste, whether it's falling to the lowest branches of life and rising from the ashes or just one of the many insignificant moments that has remained so strongly etched in our memory and our inner being that it is the culprit and catalyst in creating us as individuals. Think carefully, identify it, appreciate what happened because without it, you would be completely different people. For me, it's that aforementioned hail storm that mowed down "David's parents' crops." I wasn't even aware of that for a long time, until the moment when I could say to myself that I had finally succeeded, and then, as a revelation, I remembered this event. As if it was the driving force behind everything all these decades, but standing in the background, in silence, just enough to push in the right direction, to close the circle.

They often say that the children of the wealthy are problematic. Yes, wealthy parents can easily educate their children and provide them with all the opportunities to create their wealth. The first million is the hardest to earn, and then it somehow comes naturally. However, there is that moment that often seems to be missing in their lives—a single trauma as a catalyst, a catalyst for the creation of personality, the making of a man within us. An activator of the fight within us, a chain reaction that propels us towards the goal, towards perfection, triggering our "MAN.EXE" to operate at maximum speed and turn us into capable beings. Without that key trauma, a man's life and career often remain incomplete, not fulfilling to the extent necessary to continue stronger and more successful.

I am slowly realizing the reasons why some of the world's wealthiest people claim that they will leave all their wealth to charitable purposes rather than to their children. In fact, that is the greatest wealth they leave them—the opportunity to achieve perfection independently. Personally, I don't believe that Gates or Zuck will give away their last dollar rather than leave it to their descendants, but perhaps it is an attempt to create a catalyst for them, an awareness that one day they will be alone without a safe haven, and now is the moment to improve themselves and achieve success on their own. Sometimes I think that infamous hailstorm was the greatest gift I could receive in my childhood. Yes, I feel sorry for my parents' tears; seeing a person whom I thought was strong, tough, and everything but emotional cry due to a weather disaster carries a special weight. I cannot even imagine how much stress and suffering this event caused, but I am grateful for it because it made me who I am today.

I won't advise creating traumas for children; they naturally happen to all of us. What we can do, as men aware of our nature and basic programming, is to raise and educate our children to see beyond the rat race, not to be lured by the "piece of cheese" at the end of the maze but to create a future according to their own standards.

The role of fathers towards their male children is particularly important here. Female children just need love and pampering. I firmly stand by that, especially in the first years of their lives, and I am aware that I will teach both of them to be successful individuals from the moment they become aware of it.

Daughters are our princesses, our greatest loves. I still remember the moment when I first saw Tasa, all wrinkled, and touched those little hands for which I know I am responsible for a lifetime. Even today, her smile is something that can brighten even the worst day.

With Luka, it's slightly different, perhaps he is even more affectionate than her, but he evokes in me a special sense of father-son pride. His joy when he manages to do something crazy dangerous, yet lands on his feet, is like saying, "See, Dad, I did it!" Now that I have my own children, I don't believe it's possible to love one child more than the other, but it is possible to raise them in different ways that suit their basic human characteristics. It is our duty, in a system that seeks to turn our children into those mice from Universe 25, to create capable men and women. We can only do that if we appreciate their individuality and the diversity of genders, activating "MAN.EXE" and "woMAN.EXE" in them. Only then they will be content with what they have become, without unnatural imbalances in emotions and opinions, because a person who has experienced the love of both parents cannot be emotionally damaged, a person with an entrepreneurial spirit will not work from 9 to 5 for a miserable salary just to survive, and a person instilled with family values will not indulge in promiscuity but will want to acquire those values themselves in partners. Our duty is to provide them with a safer harbor and a warmer hearth, especially for female children, so they won't seek the lack of love in the wrong people.

Male children need special preparation. In a time when there is an obvious all-encompassing attack on masculinity as a characteristic of a good man, when the educational system is striving from an early age to destroy the family, it is especially important to provide our boys with the opportunity to be men. What does this actually mean? First of all, do not hold them back in learning their "MAN.EXE" system. Men are adventurers; their brains, bodies, hands seek nature, mud, sand, to make a sword from a tree branch, to use tools, to run, to sweat, and create a natural vent for accumulated stress. Men are truly like that, and male children should be allowed to do this often without strict control. For example, Tasa, as the first child, was, for me and my wife, initially treated with kid gloves. Apart from being a different being from Luka, more emotional and affectionate, even today, I have a stronger protective attitude towards her.

With Luka, on the other hand, I naturally allow him to fall, to "hurt himself," but every time he does something new, his determination and satisfaction with acquiring physical skills are evident in his behavior.

Allow your children to make mistakes because we ourselves don't know what the truth is. It is crucial to understand that this mistake and the "job" that the child is doing are essential for him. That climbing onto a chair is as important to him as achieving a bonus at work, for example. It provides great satisfaction, and when we remove him from the chair just before he succeeds, it creates stress in the child that needs a vent. The vent can be natural, allowing the child to explore, walk barefoot in the yard, expend all their energy by expanding knowledge and experiences, or it can be provided through cheap substitutes like phones, tablets, TVs. Then, the child becomes excessively agitated, throwing tantrums. We must bring children back to their natural environment, so strive to create your future in family homes with yards in nature, not in enclosed apartments. A park is not a substitute for a yard. Swings are not a substitute for a bow and arrow or a sword made from a piece of wood.

Female children, as beings with a pronounced emotional side, will seek their interests in different activities, naturally calmer, more empathetic, engaging in conversation and intellectual activities. Male children, on the other hand, are physically oriented. You must provide them with the opportunity to express their nature, to awaken "MAN.EXE" within them because one day, not knowing how to work with wood, various household repairs, and fieldwork will be missing in that man's differentiation as a man.

Take your son hunting, fishing, don't be afraid for him to experience some trauma by understanding that the living being he caught will be eaten because that is one of the most important elements of the basic male code. A man, by nature, is a hunter, a supplier, and if he does not accept this fact, he cannot be the man the creator made him and strive for perfection as he owes to himself, his gender, name, and ancestors.

Build your son's physical health and appearance as much as possible. Involve him in sports, martial arts, and whenever you can, involve him in physical work—mowing the grass, preparing firewood, gardening—everything that makes him stronger and more useful. If you build a physically strong and healthy man, there is a much smaller chance that he will have problematic behavior, seek a place in gangs, or abuse those weaker than himself.

Instill family values as much as possible. Be annoying at times, consciously repeat the adventures of ancestors endlessly, even if it seems like "annoying" to him now. One day, when he becomes a man, he will greatly appreciate being aware of his roots.

As a father, you are responsible for introducing your son to good habits and religion. Even if not religious, use the most basic religious principles that touch every human being. I am aware, to some extent, that religion is a product and a method of controlling subjects, but it is much more than that, as I have mentioned several times in this book.

Teach him to grow food. Teach him to cook for himself. This is perhaps one of the most important skills you can teach your son, a skill traditionally assigned to women due to generational discrimination. Preparing food, especially food we catch ourselves, is an injection of testosterone and the "MAN.EXE" system. It is the essence of our existence—catch, feed, provide.

Involve him in business as early as possible. Allow him to make mistakes, but ask for his opinion and appreciate that opinion, no matter how silly and beginner it sounds.

Build a cult of family and father's personality. Here, one should be cautious and not go to extremes. Build the cult of your personality by showing your son, through your own example, what he needs to do to be a good man.

Love his mother wholeheartedly, always be full of love, and try to make sure your children see it. There is nothing wrong with emotions, and your children need to know that. Strive to show them your emotions because you are providing an example for the future; you are setting standards that your daughter will have and your son will respect. Be a "domaćin" and involve him in everything you do in the family, in the house.

Let your children see your red lines both towards other people and towards relatives because the world is not perfect, and they will have to deal with all types of people in their lives.

Do not correct the mistakes of your parents on your children. Do not give them everything just because you had little. The values you teach them should not be derived from your parents' wrong attitudes or stubbornness but with the understanding of what kind of people you want your children to become—stable men and women, socially desirable and sought after by partners, capable individuals and at least one step more successful than you.

Be aware of your traumas and thank fate for having them because without them, you would not have become the person you are today.

Forgive! Forgive the closest ones and everybody else everything that bothered you! That is only way of forgiving yourself and growing into a person that can flower into greatness.

* * *

00:07 five months later, trying to explain why I live my purpose and the best years of my life.

A.Đ.

www.ingramcontent.com/pod-product-compliance
Lightning Source LLC
Chambersburg PA
CBHW071039290526
45795CB00004B/1228